# THE Christmas BIBLE

Heidi Tyline King

Publications International, Ltd.

Louis Weber, CEO
Publications International, Ltd.
7373 North Cicero Avenue
Lincolnwood, Illinois 60712

Permission is never granted for commercial purposes.

Manufactured in China.

8 7 6 5 4 3 2 1

ISBN: 1-4127-1209-2

Library of Congress Control Number: 2005922656

# contents

# countdown to christmas

Christmas is the most wonderful time of the year. And yet it seems like most of us spend the entire season dashing from one place to another. Between decorating, baking, and shopping, there's rarely a minute to spare. But it doesn't have to be that way. That's where *The Christmas Bible* comes in.

Within these pages, you'll find everything you need to help you prepare for the holiday season. From ideas for cards and gift wrap to decorating and party themes, we've got Christmas covered. And with more than 200 recipes to choose from, you're sure to find the perfect dishes for your yuletide gathering.

With just a little advance preparation and organization, you'll have more time to simply relax and enjoy the season. After all, isn't that what Christmas is all about?

## a word about crafts

Crafting is a wonderful way to escape the crowded shopping malls and the mad race to find the "perfect" gifts and decorations. The projects included here are for all skill levels and interests. Each project has step-by-step instructions and photos to help make everything easy to understand and fun to do.

## general pattern instructions

When a project's instructions tell you to cut out a shape according to the pattern, trace the pattern from the book onto tracing paper, using a pencil. If the pattern has an arrow with the word FOLD next to a line, it is a half pattern. Fold a sheet of tracing paper in half and open up the paper. Place the fold line of the tracing paper exactly on top of the fold line of the pattern and trace the pattern with a pencil. Then refold and cut along the line, going through both layers. Open paper for the full pattern.

## Note:

*When using heavier ribbon to make a bow, use a chenille stem to secure it. The tiny hairs on the stem will hold the bow securely and not allow the bare wire to twist. For tiny, delicate bows, use thin cloth-covered wire. It eliminates slipping and is so tiny that it disappears into the bow loops.*

Some of the patterns in this book are printed smaller than actual size. Enlarge them on a photocopier before using them, copying the pattern at the percentage indicated near the pattern.

## transferring designs

You don't have to know anything about drawing to transfer a design. The designs in this book can be transferred directly onto the project surface.

Transfer supplies: Transparent tracing paper, tape, pencil or fine-point marker, transfer paper (carbon or graphite), and stylus.

1 Place transparent tracing paper over the design you want to copy. Tape a few edges

down to hold the pattern in place. Trace the design lines with a pencil or fine-point marker. Trace only the lines you absolutely need to complete the project.

2 Place a piece of transfer paper, carbon-side down, between the object and the

pattern. Choose a color that will easily show on your project, and use a stylus or pencil to trace over the design lines. Lift a corner of the pattern to make sure the design is transferring properly.

## bows and ribbons

There are many ways to make bows, and the more you make, the easier it becomes. Cutting the ribbon ends at an angle lends a more polished appearance to the finished product.

### making a multiloop bow

1 Unroll several yards from a bolt of ribbon. Form loops from the ribbon with your

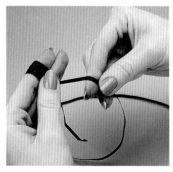

dominant hand. Pinch the center of the loops with the thumb and forefinger of your other hand as you work.

2 Continue to add loops to your bow. Keep pinching the bow's center with your thumb  and forefinger. After you have all the loops you want, trim away excess ribbon from the bolt. If you want a streamer, leave the ribbon longer before cutting.

3 Insert a length of wire through the center of the ribbon. Bring the two wire ends  securely and tightly next to the bow's center to eliminate loop slippage. Attach the bow with the wire. You may also trim the wire and glue the bow in place.

# holiday-helper calendar

## November

| | |
|---|---|
| 1–6 | Confirm holiday travel plans (airline tickets, reservations, etc.). |
| 15 | Make a master gift list for friends and family; ask for suggestions if needed. |
| 27 | Mail packages outside of the United States to ensure they arrive on time. |
| 28 | Plan holiday parties and mail invitations. |
| | Make a master list of everything that needs to be done for the holidays. |
| | Place catalog and Internet orders for gifts. |
| 30 | Mail party invitations. |

## December

| | |
|---|---|
| 1–5 | Shop for stocking stuffers and last-minute gifts. |
| | Reserve babysitters for holiday parties. |
| 4–6 | Bring home a tree. |
| 5–11 | Decorate for the holidays. |
| | Get gifts for teachers, postal carriers, and other people you want to thank. |
| 8 | Baking day—freeze goodies and pull out in batches to ensure they will last through the holidays. |
| 11 | Mail packages within the United States to ensure they arrive on time. |
| 12–14 | Plan and shop for holiday menu. |
| 12–18 | Buy, address, write, and send Christmas cards. |
| | Wrap gifts. |
| 13 | Order your ham or turkey. |
| 14 | Stock up on batteries and film. |
| 23 | Pull frozen items for holiday dinner out of the freezer. |
| 26 | Make a list of needed supplies and stock up for next year at holiday sales. |

# season's greetings

**Reaching out to others** is the perfect way to set a joyful mood for the holidays. After all, Christmas is a time for giving. Share the warmth of the season by sending beautiful, handmade Christmas cards. Or spread good cheer with thoughtful, unique gifts that come from the heart. Personalized touches—such as elegantly crafted papers and gift toppers—are certain to inspire feelings of yuletide joy.

# once upon a christmas card

Everyone loves receiving Christmas cards. Yuletide greetings help us keep family and friends close to our heart during the holidays. This year why not personalize your cards for an extra-special touch? Adding little details—family photographs, holiday newsletters, elegant handcrafted embellishments—results in lovely cards that will be cherished by all who receive them.

## effortless elegance: personalizing store-bought cards

So many of us are pressed for time during the holiday season. Try as we might, we just can't find the time to craft dozens of handmade cards. No worries. You can still add a handmade touch to your "Happy Holidays." Simply transform purchased cards into personalized holiday greetings.

If you'd like your card to feature a family photograph, purchase solid-color cards and add photographs to the front by securing with photo corners. For added interest, stamp the front of the cards with gold and silver stars, ornaments, and tree motifs. Add the same motif to the envelope for an extra touch.

You can also embellish store-bought cards by purchasing decorations that add to the design. If you're sending a limited number of greetings, consider gluing a holiday magnet to the front of cards for decoration. Look for magnets that are flat and portray a holiday scene or verse.

Decorative scrapbook embellishments are another easy way to personalize cards. Look through the selection, and mix and match Christmas decorations to affix to the front of cards. Or simply accentuate printed holiday motifs by adding glitter glue, puffy paint, and decorative stickers to cards. You don't have to be an artist; simply dot the glitter around the holiday picture.

If your purchased card is especially elegant, you might tie it with sheer, French-wire ribbon before tucking it into the envelope. Tie the ribbon into a pretty bow that lies across the front of the card.

You never get a second chance to make a first impression so don't forget the envelope! For a refined look, purchase a gold embossing kit, and add dainty details to the outside of envelopes before sending. Corners and the back flap are best for placement. For a simpler look, sprinkle decorative holiday confetti into the envelopes before sealing. Just a small shake will be sufficient to add a bit of holiday color and cheer.

## christmas cards: a history

The time-honored tradition of sending Christmas cards began about 150 years ago in Great Britain. Sir Henry Cole, a renaissance man who wrote and published books on art collections and architecture, was too busy to write customary holiday greetings to friends and family, so he asked a well-known painter to design a card with a single message that could be sent to everyone on his list.

Christmas cards popped up in the United States in the mid–1800s. In 1875, Louis Prang, who wrote and published architectural books, printed images in color with a series of lithographic zinc plates. The process allowed up to 32 colors to be printed in a single picture, with the finished product resembling an oil painting. These cards were in such high demand that Prang couldn't fill all his orders. Demand increased each year that followed, and at one point Prang was printing five million cards a year. His efforts earned him the nickname, "Father of the American Christmas Card."

The first Christmas cards featured flowers and birds, then snow scenes, fir trees, and glowing fireplaces. Today, everything from clever verse and holiday scenes to geometric designs and sports figures grace the fronts of cards.

# handcrafted cards

**Looking for a more personal** way to show how much you care? Crafting a handmade Christmas card takes so little time, yet its impact on the recipient can be profound. Try your hand at one of these quick but elegant cards.

# from our family to yours

WITH PERSONAL PICTURES ADORNING THE COVERS, THESE CARDS ARE SURE TO BE CHERISHED BY ALL WHO RECEIVE THEM.

## what you'll need

Blue art paper, cut into 10×7-inch rectangles (1 for each card)
Waxed paper
Snowflake rubber stamp
Silver pigment ink pad
Silver embossing powder
Embossing gun (or other heat source)
Extra-fine silver paint marker
Black photo corners (4 for each card)
3½×5-inch photograph (1 for each card)

1 Fold rectangles of blue paper to form 5×7-inch cards. Place card on sheet of waxed paper.

2 Apply silver ink to rubber stamp by brushing ink pad against surface of stamp.

3 Starting in a corner and working quickly but carefully, firmly press inked stamp to edge of card. Repeat around entire edge of card, reinking as necessary, to form a border of silver snowflakes. To make border look more natural, turn rubber stamp in different directions and allow some snowflakes to print off edge of card.

4 While ink is still wet, completely cover all stamped areas with embossing powder. Shake off excess powder and return to bottle.

5 Using embossing gun, heat snowflakes until powder is melted and a shiny, raised surface is formed.

6 Use paint marker to write a holiday greeting on inside of card.

7 Put photo corners on each corner of photograph. Moisten backs of photo corners and center photo on front of card, pressing down firmly.

# snapping snazzy holiday photographs

Every year it's the same story: You gather your family together and spend the better part of an afternoon taking pictures for your Christmas card. Yet despite your best efforts, the outcome is discouraging: red eyes, startled expressions, fuzzy family members. Don't despair! With a few photography pointers, you'll go from pressured to pro in no time.

**Read the instructions.** Few people sit down and read the instruction manual accompanying their camera, yet taking time out to do so can save you film and hassle. Not only does the guide explain optimal settings for specific shots, it also clarifies the use of each button and knob.

**Digitize the outcome.** If you are using a digital camera, set the output to the recommended settings. This helps with focus, centering, and printing.

**Increase your film speed.** If you are a novice photographer, ASA 400 film works best. If you are using a digital camera, set the ASA to 200 or 400.

**Prepare your subjects.** For group shots, coordinated dress gives pictures a professional touch. Stay away from checks and plaids, which tend to make a shot busy. Instead, opt for solid colors, and remember that light colors will appear crisp in a photograph.

**Be candid.** Go for a few posed shots, but keep in mind the best photographs capture true emotion. Have your family stack on top of one another in a pyramid, scrunch together on a tree swing, or crouch in a football huddle. Any activity where you are together in a spontaneous way has the potential to produce fantastic photos.

**Choose the right light.** Believe it or not, overcast days often produce the best outdoor pictures. That's because there are no shadows or bright rays of light falling across your subjects, making them dark or causing them to squint. Try to plan your shoots early in the morning or just before dusk when the light is softer.

**Start early.** Waiting until the last minute to get your holiday photo will only make the situation more stressful. Schedule a time about a month in advance to get your shot. If you aren't happy with the outcome, you can retake your pictures in time to put cards in the mail.

**Watch your back.** When taking pictures, pay special attention to what you see in the background. Try to position subjects in front of a stationary background such as a grove of trees or on porch steps to keep unnecessary movement from interfering with the shot.

# sending holiday wishes

MAKING HOLIDAY GREETING CARDS TO SEND TO YOUR LOVED ONES TELLS THEM HOW MUCH YOU LOVE THEM—OFTEN BETTER THAN MERE WORDS CAN EVER CONVEY!

## what you'll need

15¾×5¼-inch piece white paper (1 for each card)
Ruler
Pencil
Scissors
⅛-inch hole punch
7¼×5¼-inch piece black paper (1 for each card)
Craft glue
Green paper, 7×5 inches each (2 for each card)
Scrap yellow paper

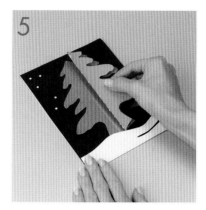

1 Fold a short end of the white paper up to create a 1¼-inch flap. Fold remaining length of paper in half to form a card.

2 Trace the snowbank pattern onto flap. Cut out snowbank shape.

3 Punch 8 holes in black paper with hole punch, leaving middle of card for tree placement. Glue black paper to front of card.

4 Trace tree pattern onto each piece of green paper. Cut out tree shapes. Fold each tree in half lengthwise.

5 Glue a tree to middle of card, above snowbank flap. Glue fold of other tree on fold line of glued-down tree.

6 Cut star from yellow paper, and glue at top of tree.

*Enlarge patterns 125%*

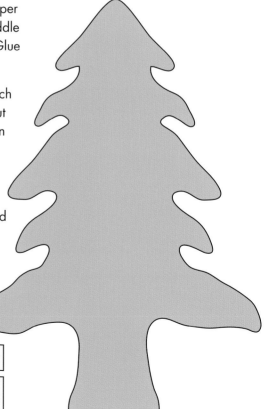

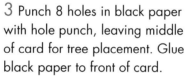

## read all about it

The holidays are a great time to catch up with family and friends. One of the best ways to stay in touch is to write a family newsletter detailing events of the prior year. With so many graphic design computer programs on the market, the process has never been easier.

The first step is to actually sit down and think about the past year, month by month, jotting down important dates and hallmark moments. The big events come easiest: birthdays, graduations, promotions, vacations, and moves. Equally important are the small but telling events that happen to all of us: a baby's first steps, a teenager getting their driver's license, the addition of a new pet, learning a new hobby.

When you have an outline, consult with your family and encourage them to write down memories of their own. Someone might have an interesting story to tell about school, while another might talk about their favorite food. It doesn't really matter what the subject is as long as it reveals a personal side to the person.

When you have all your information in hand, sit down and write your letter. Use the months as a way to break up the text, or tell about each family member in a separate paragraph. Don't worry if you do not like to write. Instead make lists, such as favorite moments, funniest events, and best night out. If you will be including photographs in your newsletter, use captions to help tell the story. This way, you can emphasize the year's highlights.

Another way to spice up your holiday newsletter is to get creative with your design. You don't have to put your newsletter in straight letter form. Instead, write in tidbits, print them out, then cut and paste them onto the page, interspersing photos and clip art for illustrations.

## displaying holiday cards

So many cards . . . so little time to enjoy them. This year, instead of stacking them on a table or in a corner where you'll never see them, use the cards as part of your holiday decorating.

One of the easiest ways to display cards is to purchase a bulletin board and paint it with Christmas colors or a holiday motif. For a festive touch, glue decorative stars to the tops of flat thumbtacks and use them to hang the cards.

Another idea is to fold an 8-foot-long, 2-inch-wide ribbon in half. Clip the ends to prevent raveling, and secure the folded top to the wall with thumbtacks or small brads. Tape your holiday cards down each piece of ribbon, leaving enough room in between to see the front of each card.

If you have a flat coffee table that will lend itself to displays, purchase a piece of glass cut the same size as the top of your table. Make sure the edges have been polished to prevent cuts. Then slip your cards underneath the glass to enjoy throughout the holiday season. You may even want to display your cards all year long!

A pretty screen in the corner of a living room is the perfect place to showcase special cards. Line them up, or scatter them across the surface for a less formal look.

If you would like to display your photograph Christmas cards all year, slip the cards into flat plastic frames with magnets on the back and display them on your refrigerator. You'll be surprised how much families change from year to year.

For a display across your mantel or buffet, take a piece of string and

*Special Christmas cards from loved ones signify the meaning of the season. To keep heartfelt sentiments close at hand during the holidays, clip your cards to a small Christmas tree or pine branch.*

## all wrapped up!

Giving is what makes Christmas such a heartwarming season. So much time and care is spent selecting the "perfect" gift for those on our list. But what about the packaging? How a package looks on the outside sets the tone for the gift inside, and a splendidly wrapped package illustrates the love and care that went into the selection of the gift. With just a few simple touches, you can wrap your special presents with style. After all, what could be more fun than giving a gift wrapped from the heart?

attach it to each side. Using paper clips or miniature clothespins, secure cards to the string, equally spacing to keep the weight balanced.

Handmade cards are especially charming. To display those with unique details or personal significance, find a small frame with a ready-made mat and slip the card inside for an elegant display.

*An antique-style office organizer makes a handy container for holiday gift wrap items. Storing your gift embellishments close at hand makes wrapping a snap!*

# stylish box toppers

**The package toppers** on the following pages are fun to make—and quick to impress. Follow the easy instructions to make sophisticated embellishments for your presents.

# groomed in velvet

NOTHING SAYS ELEGANCE
LIKE VELVET. A GIFT THIS BEAUTIFUL
IS SURE TO STAND OUT
UNDER THE TREE!

## what you'll need

1 yard of 60-inch-wide midnight blue velvet,
   cut into a 31×31-inch piece and a 15×15-inch piece

10×10×9-inch rigid gift box with top and bottom

All-purpose craft glue

Scissors

One 3- to 4-inch plastic foam flower arranger

4½ yards of 2-inch-wide gold wire-edged nylon ribbon,
   cut into one 2-yard and two 1¼-yard lengths

Assorted dusty rose and blue silk flowers

2 bunches of artificial blue or dusty rose grapes

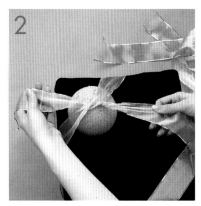

1 Place the 31×31-inch piece of velvet on your work surface, wrong-side up. Drizzle a line of glue around the outer edges of the box bottom. Center the bottom on top of the velvet. Wrap the bottom, using the craft glue to secure the velvet to the inside of the box. Trim extra fabric as needed when executing folds. Allow to dry. Repeat using 15×15-inch piece of velvet and the top of the box. Allow to dry.

2 Place box right-side up. Glue the flower arranger on the top-left corner of the box. Place 2-yard piece of ribbon over the bottom-right corner of the box with equal lengths extending. Pass the ends under the bottom-left and top-right corners. Bring the ends up together at the top-left corner over the flower arranger. Tie them tightly into a single knot over the flower arranger to secure.

3 Press ends of flowers and grapes into flower arranger. Trim ribbon ends. Pass 1¼-yard ribbon length under first knot. Bring ends together. Tie into a bow over first knot. Repeat using remaining ribbon.

# the holly and the ivy

'TIS THE SEASON FOR HOLLY AND IVY. THIS PACKAGE TOPPER IS CHRISTMAS AT ITS BEST!

## what you'll need

7×7×7-inch gift box

Copper moiré medium-weight wrapping paper, cut into a 30×16-inch sheet

Double-sided tape

3 yards of 1½-inch-wide teal wired silk ribbon, moiré ribbon, or satin ribbon, divided into 2⅓-yard and ⅔-yard lengths

1¾-inch plastic foam flower arranger

All-purpose craft glue

Silk variegated ivy sprigs or fresh variegated ivy sprigs

Artificial red berries and pinecone boughs or individual holly boughs and small pinecones

1 Wrap the box using the wrapping paper and double-sided tape. Turn the package upside-down. Place the 2⅓-yard ribbon length under the box with equal lengths extending. Bring the ends together at the center and cross them, pulling them tightly in opposite directions. Bring the ends toward the top of the package, holding them securely in place. Turn the package right-side up. Center the flower arranger on top of the package, and secure using craft glue. Allow to dry. Tie the ends into a bow, securing the flower arranger. Crinkle ribbon ends.

2 Press the ends of the ivy, red berries, and pinecones into the plastic foam arranger as desired.

3 Tie the remaining ⅔-yard of ribbon into a loose single knot over the first knot. Trim the ends as desired.

# elegant wire ornaments

SPREAD THE JOY OF
CHRISTMAS WITH THESE
SIMPLE YET ELEGANT
DECORATIONS. WHAT
COULD BE BETTER THAN
A PACKAGE TOPPER
THAT DOUBLES AS AN
ORNAMENT?

## what you'll need

36-inch length 18-gauge steel spool wire
Needle-nose pliers
Wire cutters
2 beads
14 inches silver cord

1 Use needle-nose pliers to bend wire into letter shapes, using one of the patterns for a guide. Trim excess wire with wire cutters.

2 Slip bead onto each end of wire. Use pliers to make small loop at end of the wire to prevent bead from slipping off.

3 Fold the cord in half, and knot the loose ends. Tie cord around the top of the letter O for hanger.

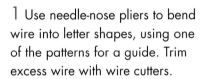

*Enlarge patterns 166%*

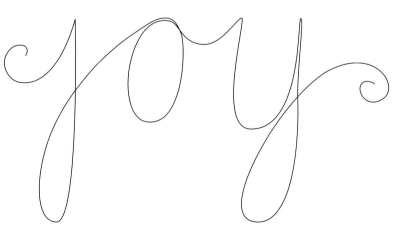

# snowflakes aglitter

BRING THE SPARKLE OF WINTER INTO YOUR HOME WITH THESE STUNNING SNOWFLAKES. ADD THEM TO A PRESENT FOR AN EXTRA-SPECIAL TOUCH!

## what you'll need

#28 silver beading wire

Tape measure

Wire cutters

Small snowflake: 30 seed beads (A); 24 accent beads (B); 6 bugle beads

Medium snowflake: 56 seed beads (A); 12 large accent beads (B); 6 bugle beads

Large snowflake: 48 seed beads (A); 24 large accent beads (B); 6 bugle beads (about ½ inch long); 18 shorter bugle beads (about ⅜ inch long)

1 jump ring for each snowflake

18 inches satin ribbon for each snowflake, ⅛ inch wide

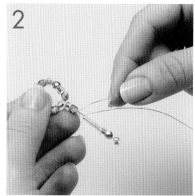

## small snowflake

1 Cut 28 inches of wire. Thread on 1 bead A and 1 bead B 6 times. Bend wire to form a circle, and feed end of wire through beads again. Leave a small tail on one end, which will be used to tighten circle; end will be worked into finished snowflake.

2 Place beads on long tail of wire in this order: 1 bead A, 1 bead B, 1 bugle, 1 bead A, 1 bead B, 1 bead A. Bend wire around the last bead, and thread it back through 2 beads and bugle. Pull wire tight, enclosing end bead on point.

3 Place 1 bead B and 1 bead A on wire. Insert through bead A on center circle, and pull tight.

4 Repeat steps 2 and 3 five more times. Insert jump ring into top of last point of snowflake. Work tails of wire into beading, and clip extra wire. Tie ribbon onto jump ring.

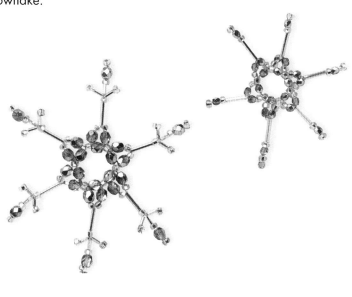

*snowflakes aglitter* continued

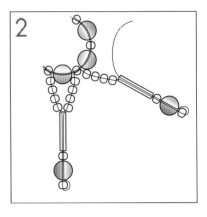

## medium snowflake

1 Cut 36 inches of wire. Thread on 1 bead A and 1 bead B 6 times. Bend wire to form a circle, and feed end of wire through beads again. Leave a small tail on one end, which will be used to tighten circle; end will be worked into finished snowflake.

2 Place beads on long tail of wire in this order: 4 bead A, 1 bugle, 1 bead A, 1 bead B, 1 bead A. Bend wire around last bead, and feed it through next 2 beads and bugle. Pull wire tight, enclosing end bead on point.

3 Place 4 bead A on wire. Insert wire through bead A on center circle, and pull tight.

4 Repeat steps 2 and 3 five more times. Insert jump ring into top of last point of snowflake. Work tails of wire into beading, and clip extra wire. Tie ribbon onto jump ring.

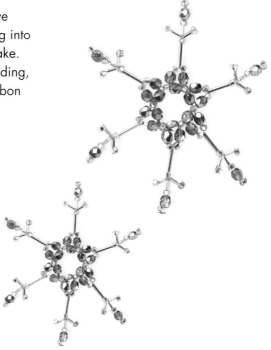

# large snowflake

1 Repeat step 1 of medium snowflake, but use 42 inches of wire.

2 Place beads on long tail of wire in this order: 1 bead B, 1 bead A, 1 long bugle, 1 bead A, 1 short bugle, 1 bead A. Bend wire over last bead, and feed it back through short bugle. Pull wire tight. Place 1 short bugle, 1 bead A, 1 bead B, 1 bead A on wire. Bend wire around last bead, and insert it back through 2 beads and bugle. Pull wire tight. Place 1 short bugle and 1 bead A on wire. Bring the wire over the end bead and back through bugle. Pull wire tight. Feed wire back through bead A and long bugle bead.

3 Place 1 bead A and 1 bead B on wire. Insert wire through bead A in center circle, and pull tight.

4 Repeat steps 2 and 3 five more times. Insert jump ring into top of last point on snowflake. Work tails of wire into beading, and clip extra wire. Tie ribbon onto jump ring.

*Keep your package decorations in one central location. When it's time to wrap, everything will be at your fingertips!*

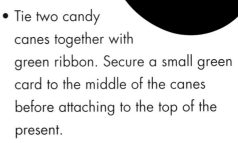

## gift tags in a snap!

A pretty gift tag transforms a present. Handmade tags are unique, inexpensive, and easy to make. And they're a fun way to add a personal touch to your gift. Use the suggestions below to get started:

- Make color photocopies of elegant fabric and cut into small rectangles for tags. Punch a hole in the corner and add a pretty ribbon to finish.
- Copy photographs onto sticker paper and cut out, leaving white space at the bottom of the photo to write "To" and "From."

- Purchase small round Christmas balls, and write the recipient's name on the ball with a metallic pen. Secure to the present with ribbon.
- Tie two candy canes together with green ribbon. Secure a small green card to the middle of the canes before attaching to the top of the present.
- Print tags on heavy paper in a fancy font, then cut them out with decorative-cut scissors.
- Recycle gorgeous gift wrap by cutting it into larger-than-usual gift tags. If the paper is too thin to use alone, glue it to the front of card stock, or cut around motifs and glue them to the cards.
- Mount a gift card on the top of a box using photo corners. These not only look elegant, but they make the card the focal point of the present.

# paper magic

**A gift that is beautifully wrapped** can turn the simplest present into a grand gift. The following handmade gift wraps require little skill or time, and their techniques can be adapted to use as a jumping-off point to create customized designs. Your gifts will be the prettiest ones under the tree!

# silver and gold

THE RICH LOOK OF THIS
HAND-PAINTED WRAPPING PAPER
IS SIMPLE TO ACHIEVE.
SUCH UNDERSTATED ELEGANCE
IS BOUND TO MAKE AN IMPACT
UNDER THE TREE!

## what you'll need

Cream 90-pound water-color paper, cut into a 23×12½-inch sheet
Silver and gold acrylic paints
Disposable foil containers
2 paintbrushes, approximately 1¼ inches wide
6×6×4½-inch gift box
Double-sided tape
2 yards of 1½-inch-wide wire-edged silver nylon ribbon cut into
    two 1-yard lengths
2 yards of 1½-inch-wide wire-edged gold nylon ribbon cut into
    two 1-yard lengths
Green floral wire
1 gold or silver pinecone or ball ornament

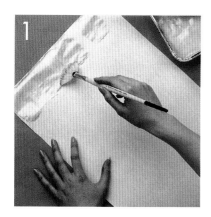

1 Cover work surface with cardboard. Put paper, right-side up, on cardboard. Place small amount of silver paint in a disposable foil container. Thin with water until mixture is the consistency of heavy cream. Repeat with gold paint. Dip a brush into the paint. Starting at the upper corner of the paper, paint silver daubs every two inches using quick brushstrokes. Using the gold, fill in between the silver strokes. Repeat the rows, alternating the starting color, until paper is covered. Allow to dry.

2 Turn paper wrong-side up, wrap box using double-sided tape, then turn box right-side up. Slightly overlap one silver and one gold ribbon, placing them under the box with equal lengths extending. Bring ends together at the center and tie in a knot. Pass end of remaining gold ribbon under first knot. Bring ends together and tie into a bow over the first knot. Repeat using remaining silver ribbon. Place small piece of floral wire around the pinecone. Attach it to the knot in the center of the bows.

# snowflake wrapping paper

THE DELICATE PATTERN OF SNOWFLAKES WILL GENERATE A BLIZZARD OF COMPLIMENTS! ONCE YOU'VE CUT OUT THE SNOWFLAKES, YOU CAN MAKE MANY DIFFERENT VERSIONS— THINK OF ALL THE POSSIBILITIES.

## what you'll need

12 to 15 squares of paper,
    about 4½ square inches each
Scissors
Iron
White wrapping paper
Plastic snowflakes (optional)
Blue spray paint

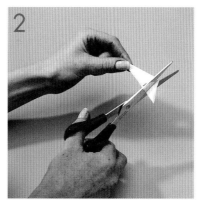

4 In a well-ventilated area, arrange snowflakes on white paper so they overlap slightly. If you have plastic snowflakes, use them to weigh down paper ones.

5 Shake can of paint well before spraying lightly over paper, using gentle back and forth motion. Hold can high off paper, and spray from directly above to avoid moving snowflakes. Allow to dry for a few minutes so you don't smudge paint when you remove snowflakes. Snowflakes can be reused.

1 Start with a square of paper. Fold the bottom edge of your square up to the top edge to make a rectangle. Fold this rectangle in half so you have a square. Fold this square from corner to corner to create a triangle.

2 With the single fold at the bottom, fold down side with several creases to touch bottom edge. Cut off the paper that hangs off the end.

3 Now you're ready to cut designs in the paper. Some designs can be cut on the side with the single fold, but don't cut it away completely or snowflake will fall apart. Experiment with cutting out diamonds, circles, and odd shapes from the multi-creased side. Unfold paper. Cut 12 to 15 snowflakes. Iron them so they lie flat. Iron sheets of white paper.

# noel gift wrap and tag

BUNDLE YOUR GIFTS IN AN
ARRAY OF TOUCH-OF-GOLD
HOLLY LEAVES ON HIGH-
GLOSS PAPER. A GOLD
FRENCH-WIRE RIBBON
COMPLETES THIS ELEGANT
LOOK.

## what you'll need

White high-gloss gift wrap paper
Embossing ink and pad
Holly sprig stamp
Gold embossing powder
Embossing gun
Double-sided tape
Gold French-wire ribbon
White high-gloss gift tag

1 Unroll enough gift wrap paper
to cover your gift box. Working
on one section of paper at a
time, use embossing ink to stamp
the gift wrap with the holly sprig
stamp. Be sure to reink the stamp
after each impression.

2 Sprinkle the images with gold embossing powder, tapping excess powder back into the jar.

3 Use the embossing gun to melt the embossing powder. Be careful not to burn the paper.

4 Wrap your gift and tie it with the gold French-wire ribbon.

5 Stamp the holly sprig along the top and bottom edges of the gift tag.

6 Sprinkle with embossing powder and heat with the embossing gun as in steps 2 and 3.

## *packing gifts for holiday mailing*

Do long lines, fees for express delivery, and the stress of last-minute errands sound like things you'd rather avoid? Then get organized—get your holiday packages out before the crowd.

Mail packages no later than December 10 if you're planning on ground shipping. International mailings should go out by the first of the month for delivery before the holidays, and no later than December 12 for express delivery. If you plan to use first-class and priority mail, get domestic packages to the post office by the second week in December. For exact dates, visit the Web site for the shipper you plan to use.

Sturdy boxes are essential. Once you have added your gifts, fill the box with packing material such as Styrofoam popcorn, peanuts, or crumpled newspaper. Wrap breakable items separately before wrapping in gift wrap for a double layer of protection. If you are using a recycled box, make sure the address and return address are prominently displayed—there should be no other readable addresses on the box. Label the box "perishable" or "breakable" if appropriate, and seal with several wraps of packing tape.

If you order gifts online, take advantage of free shipping offers. You won't have to mail the present yourself, and if it arrives broken, a replacement will be sent free of charge.

Check with your shipper before purchasing insurance. Some provide up to $100 coverage automatically. Homeowner's insurance might also cover shipping mishaps.

*Looking for a thoughtful gift for your entertainer? Consider a pretty plant displayed in a painted bucket and tied with a bow, decorative holiday bowls stacked and filled with nuts or candy, or simple glass pillars embellished with holly.*

## gifting the host

Holidays mean parties, and parties mean thank-you gifts for your hosts. This year, plan ahead and have a few on hand.

Wine is always a good gift—look for a bottle with a special holiday label or flavor. Wrap the wine in a pretty bag for a glamorous presentation that's sure to impress.

Candles are festive gifts. Spiff up pillar candles by tying a pretty ribbon around them. Votives look nice grouped in threes and matched with nice votive holders. Tapers can be tied together and presented with a wrapped box of matches.

Gift soaps are lovely treasures that we hesitate to buy for ourselves. Purchase a box of several, and wrap them individually when you need a quick present. Pair them with a holiday hand towel for an extra thoughtful gift.

Who doesn't like getting a box of their favorite candies? A small box with sumptuous chocolates works as well as a larger one with a less-than-appealing assortment.

Picture frames with a photo of you and the host or a thank-you note inside show that you put thought into your selection.

Holiday music CDs are always appreciated, as are bath salts and oils in a soothing scent. What a perfect way for your host to unwind after the party!

Coasters make a lovely present. Select ones that match your host's décor or that have a holiday theme.

# it's in the bag

**Looking for an extra special way** to wrap that thank-you gift? Check out some of these handmade packaging ideas. Who can help but be flattered that you spent so much time and effort? Recipients don't need to know how fun and easy these projects are to create!

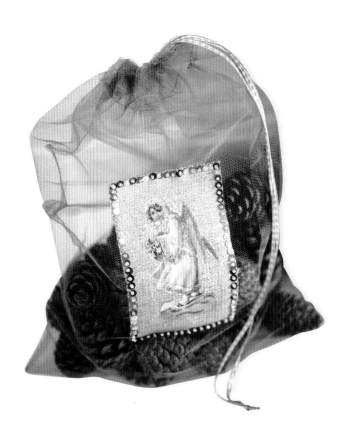

# sponged gift bags

USE A FEW SPONGES AND SOME GLEAMING PAINTS TO TURN YOUR PLAIN BROWN WRAPPER INTO A WONDERFUL WORK OF ART. YOUR CRAFTING WILL BE APPRECIATED AS MUCH AS THE GIFT INSIDE!

## what you'll need

3 pieces household sponge, 1×1½ inches each
Paper plates
Metallic paint: royal ruby, crystal green, glorious gold
Brown paper bag in desired size
Hole punch
1 yard ribbon, ⅜ inch wide
6 jingle bells, 12mm each
Scissors

1 Moisten pieces of sponge; squeeze out excess water.

2 Pour a small amount of royal ruby paint onto paper plate. Dip sponge into paint and dab off excess on clean area of paper plate. Open bag. Place hand and arm into bag, and lightly sponge ruby paint onto all sides, using your hand inside of bag to give support as needed. Repeat with green and then gold paint. Allow bag to dry.

3 Punch holes about 1 inch or so apart around top of bag.

4 Weave ribbon through holes, threading a jingle bell onto each section of ribbon that will remain outside of bag.

5 Insert gift into bag and carefully pull ribbon ends to gather top of bag. Tie into a bow and thread bells onto each ribbon end, securing with a knot.

# regal vintage

## what you'll need

15×9-inch rectangular bag pattern (see page 45)

⅓ yard midnight blue (or desired jewel tone) silk taffeta

Midnight blue thread

⅓ yard burgundy (or desired jewel tone) silk taffeta

Burgundy thread

Scissors

Iron

Gift bottle

1¼ yards 2-inch-wide copper wire-edged nylon ribbon

1 Enlarge the pattern on page 45 using the dimensions provided and transfer to lightweight cardboard or tracing paper. Using both taffeta pieces, cut 2 patterns for each color. Working with the 2 blue pieces, match the right sides together. Using a ½-inch seam allowance and thread to match the fabric, sew the sides and bottom of the bag together. Repeat using the burgundy pieces. Turn the bags right-side out.

2 Press the seams. Match the side seams at the top of the bag. Using a ½-inch seam allowance and midnight blue thread, sew around the tops of bags, leaving a 3-inch gap for turning the burgundy bag. Turn the burgundy bag right-side out. You should end up with the burgundy bag on one side and the midnight blue bag on the other.

3 Push the burgundy bag inside the blue bag. Whipstitch the opening to close.

4 For giving, place the desired wine in the bag. Tie the ribbon into a bow around the top of the filled bag. Crimp the wire ribbon ends as desired.

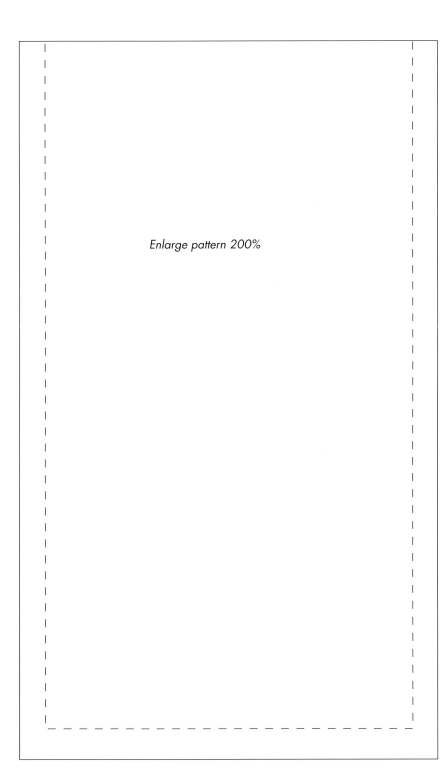

Enlarge pattern 200%

## wrapping options

Want to create an elegant effect without sewing? If you're short on sewing time, you can achieve the same stunning looks with a deep blue or violet bottle bag available in card and party stores. Adorn with a satiny peach, copper, or burgundy bow and you're set.

For another option, check out your scrap fabric pile. Select a richly colored floral or plaid. Cut the fabric into a square approximately 22×22 inches. Place the desired bottle in the center and bundle the fabric around the bottle. Tie a contrasting ribbon around the neck to complete the look.

# see-through surprise gift bags

GIVE A SPECIAL TREATMENT WITH THESE BEAUTIFUL HANDMADE BAGS. AN ORGANDY WINDOW PROVIDES A SNEAK PEEK AT THE GIFT INSIDE. THEY'RE SO SIMPLE TO MAKE, YOU CAN EASILY CREATE GIFT BAGS IN ANY SIZE OR FABRIC COMBINATION.

## what you'll need

12×45 inches velvet or other fabric
Ruler
Pencil
Scissors
7×5 inches organdy
Straight pins
Sewing machine
Thread to match
2 yards decorative ribbon, ¼ to ½ inch wide
Needle
4 large decorative beads

**1**

**2**

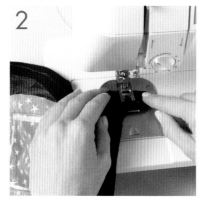

**3**

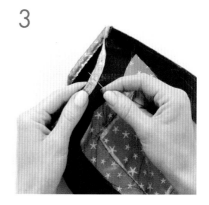

1 Cut two 8½×9½-inch rectangles from main fabric. Make "window" in 1 fabric piece by cutting 3×4-inch rectangle in center. On wrong side of fabric, cover opening with organdy; pin in place. With right side up, sew organdy to fabric along cut edge. Baste decorative ribbon around organdy window to cover seam. Sew in place, and remove basting stitches.

2 With right sides facing, pin and then stitch sides and bottom of fabric pieces together. Fold bottom corners flat, and sew a line across about ¾ inch from corner edge. Turn inside out.

3 Sew ribbon along top of bag, then fold it over to inside of bag opening. Hand-sew other edge of ribbon in place.

4 To make handles, cut four 7-inch lengths of ribbon. Place 2 lengths on top of each other, and sew along edges. Repeat for other 2 lengths. Slip 2 beads on each handle, and pin handles to bag opening. Sew in place.

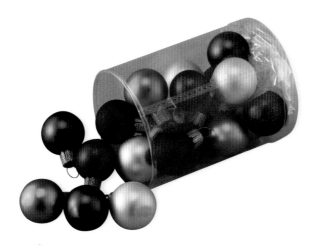

# gifts from a jar

**Short on time** and money? No problem. With a few simple ingredients and some scraps of material, you can create inexpensive jar mixes that never fail to delight. The idea is simple: Combine the mix ingredients in a decorative gift jar and create a gift tag with the recipe that will be used to complete the treat. The recipient then empties the jar into a bowl, follows the attached recipe, and voilà— a savory or sweet treat that mixes up in minutes.

# o christmas tree

## what you'll need

Flat-topped 1½-quart glass or
    acrylic jar
Food gift
One 6- to 8-inch miniature
    artificial Christmas tree
Hot glue gun and glue sticks or
    all-purpose craft glue
2 to 3 miniature holiday gifts
Miniature tree decorations
    (star, lights, ornaments, garlands)
Green floral wire
1 yard of 2½-inch-wide
    Christmas ribbon

1 Fill the jar with the food gift as
desired. Close or seal the jar.
Center the tree on top of the lid
and attach with the hot glue gun
or craft glue. Allow to dry.

2 Glue the gifts under the tree
as desired. Allow to dry. Decorate the tree as desired, attaching ornaments with floral wire.

3 To make the bow, circle the
ribbon around the lid. Tie the
ends into a loose knot. Trim the
ends as desired.

# crispy holiday treats mix

**1 cup powdered sugar**
**1½ cups crisp rice cereal**
**½ cup chopped dried tart cherries**
**¾ cup mini semisweet chocolate chips**
**¼ cup chopped toasted pecans**
**¾ cup flaked coconut**

1. Layer all ingredients except coconut attractively in any order in 1-quart food storage jar with tight-fitting lid. (Pack ingredients down firmly before adding another layer.) Place coconut in small plastic food storage bag. Close with twist tie; cut off top of bag. Place bag in jar.

2. Cover top of jar with 8-inch circle of fabric; attach recipe gift tag with raffia or ribbon. *Makes 1 (1-quart) jar*

**Gift Idea:** Assemble a holiday gift bag with a jar of Crispy Holiday Treats Mix, a package of small paper or foil candy cups, and a decorative candy dish. Candy cups are available in a variety of designs and colors at stores that carry cake decorating supplies.

# crispy holiday treats

**1 jar Crispy Holiday Treats Mix**
**1 cup peanut butter**
**¼ cup (½ stick) butter, softened**

1. Remove coconut packet from jar. Place remaining contents of jar in large bowl; stir to blend. Combine peanut butter and butter in medium bowl, stirring until well blended. Add to cereal mixture. Stir until well blended.

2. Shape generous teaspoonfuls of dough into 1½-inch balls. Roll balls in coconut. Place in single layer in large food storage container. Store in refrigerator.

*Makes about 2 dozen treats*

*crispy holiday treats mix*

# festive cranberry waffles mix

**¾ cup all-purpose flour**
**2 teaspoons baking powder**
**1 teaspoon dried orange peel**
**½ teaspoon baking soda**
**½ teaspoon ground cinnamon**
**¼ teaspoon salt**
**⅓ cup yellow cornmeal**
**⅓ cup sugar**
**½ cup dried cranberries or dried cherries, coarsely chopped**
**¼ cup all-purpose flour**

1. Layer all ingredients in order listed above in 1-pint food storage jar with tight-fitting lid. (Pack ingredients down lightly before adding another layer.)

2. Cover top of jar with 8-inch circle of fabric; attach recipe gift tag with raffia or ribbon. *Makes 1 (1-pint) jar*

**GIFT-GIVING TIP:** Assemble a brunch gift basket with a jar of Festive Cranberry Waffles Mix, a bottle of maple syrup, a package of gourmet ground coffee, and 8 juice oranges. For a more elaborate holiday gift, add a waffle iron.

## festive cranberry waffles

**1 jar Festive Cranberry Waffles Mix**
**1 cup buttermilk**
**¼ to ½ cup milk or orange juice, divided**
**1 egg**
**1 teaspoon vanilla**
**3 tablespoons butter, melted**
**Toppings: Butter, maple syrup, and powdered sugar (optional)**

1. Preheat waffle iron.

2. Place contents of jar in large bowl; stir until well blended. Whisk together buttermilk, ¼ cup milk, egg, and vanilla in medium bowl. Add to flour mixture; stir until just moistened. Stir in butter. Add additional milk, 1 tablespoon at a time, if batter is too thick.

*continued on page 54*

*festive cranberry waffles*

## helpful hint

*festive cranberry waffles,* continued

3. Spray waffle iron with nonstick cooking spray. Spoon about ¾ cup batter* onto iron. Close lid; bake until steaming stops or waffles are brown and crispy. Serve immediately with desired toppings.          *Makes 4 (7-inch) round waffles*

*\*Check the waffle iron's manufacturer's directions for the recommended amount of batter and baking time.*

**TIP:** Waffles can be made in advance, then cooled, wrapped, and frozen. Reheat frozen waffles in a toaster or toaster oven.

**SERVING SUGGESTION:** Combine 1 cup mascarpone cheese, ¼ cup maple syrup, and 1 teaspoon vanilla until well mixed. Serve in place of butter and syrup.

# hot & spicy mustard

**¼ cup water**
**¼ cup whole yellow mustard seeds**
**¼ cup honey**
**3 tablespoons cider vinegar**
**2 tablespoons ground mustard**
**1 teaspoon salt**
**⅛ teaspoon ground cloves**

1. Place water in small saucepan. Bring to a boil over high heat. Add mustard seeds. Cover saucepan; remove from heat. Let stand 1 hour or until liquid is absorbed.

2. Spoon mustard seeds into work bowl of food processor.

3. Add honey, vinegar, ground mustard, salt, and cloves to work bowl; process using on/off pulsing action until mixture is thickened and seeds are coarsely chopped, scraping down side of work bowl once with spatula. Refrigerate at least 1 day before serving.

4. Store in airtight container in refrigerator up to 3 weeks.

*Makes about 1 cup*

# cocoa brownies mix

**1¼ cups all-purpose flour**
**1 cup granulated sugar**
**¾ cup packed light brown sugar**
**⅔ cup unsweetened cocoa powder**
**½ cup chopped walnuts**
**1 teaspoon baking powder**
**¼ teaspoon salt**

1. Layer ingredients attractively in any order in 1-quart food storage jar with tight-fitting lid. (Pack ingredients down firmly before adding another layer.)

2. Cover top of jar with 8-inch circle of fabric; attach recipe gift tag with raffia or ribbon. *Makes 1 (1-quart) jar*

## cocoa brownies

**¾ cup (1½ sticks) butter, softened**
**3 eggs**
**1½ teaspoons vanilla**
**1 jar Cocoa Brownies Mix**

1. Preheat oven to 350°F. Lightly grease 13×9-inch baking pan.

2. Beat butter in large bowl until smooth. Beat in eggs and vanilla until blended. (Mixture may appear curdled.) Add brownie mix to butter mixture; stir until well blended.

3. Spread batter evenly in prepared pan. Bake 20 to 25 minutes or until brownies spring back when lightly touched. Do not overbake. Cool in pan on wire rack.
*Makes about 2½ dozen brownies*

# lithuanian christmas bread mix

**2½ cups flour**
**¼ cup poppy seeds**
**1 teaspoon salt**
**1½ cups golden raisins**

1. Mix flour, poppy seeds, and salt in large bowl. Layer flour mixture and raisins in 1-quart food storage jar with tight-fitting lid. (Pack ingredients down lightly before adding another layer.)

2. Cover top of jar with 8-inch circle of fabric; attach recipe gift tag with raffia or ribbon. *Makes 1 (1-quart) jar*

## lithuanian christmas bread

**1¼ cups milk**
**¼ cup (½ stick) butter**
**3 tablespoons honey**
**1 jar Lithuanian Christmas Bread Mix**
**1 packet quick-rise active dry yeast**
**Additional honey for glaze**

1. Grease 9×5×3-inch loaf pan. Combine milk, butter, and honey in small saucepan. Heat over low heat until temperature reaches 130°F (just under a simmer). Pour contents of jar into large bowl. Stir in dry yeast. Pour hot liquid into bowl and stir to form rough dough. Transfer dough to prepared pan. Let rise in warm place 1 hour or until doubled in bulk.

2. Preheat oven to 350°F. Bake 45 minutes or until loaf springs back when touched in center. Brush with additional honey during last 5 minutes of baking to glaze. Cool; remove from pan. Slice into thin slices; serve. *Makes 1 loaf*

# mocha espresso mix

**4 ounces semisweet chocolate (squares or bars)**
**¾ cup nonfat dry milk powder**
**½ cup espresso powder**
**½ teaspoon ground cinnamon**

1. Place chocolate on cutting board; shave into small pieces with paring knife.

2. Combine chocolate, dry milk powder, espresso powder, and cinnamon in small bowl until well blended.

3. Spoon mixture into clean, dry decorative glass food storage jar with tight-fitting lid. Cover top of jar with 8-inch circle of fabric; attach recipe gift tag with raffia or ribbon.

4. Store at room temperature up to 1 month.          *Makes about 1⅔ cups mix*

# mocha espresso

**2 tablespoons Mocha Espresso Mix**
**6 ounces boiling water**
   **Whipped cream (optional)**

Spoon espresso mix into cup or mug. Add boiling water; stir. Serve with whipped cream, if desired.          *Makes 1 serving*

## helpful hint

*Vinegars can be used in salad dressings, marinades, and sweet-and-sour sauces. They may also be used for preserving and pickling.*

# herbed vinegar

**1½ cups white wine vinegar**
**½ cup fresh basil leaves**

1. Pour vinegar into nonaluminum 2-quart saucepan. Heat until very hot, stirring occasionally. Do not boil. (If vinegar boils, it will become cloudy.)

2. Pour into glass bowl; add basil. Cover with plastic wrap. Refrigerate about 1 week or until desired amount of flavor develops. Store in food storage jar or bottle with tight-fitting lid in refrigerator up to 6 months.

*Makes about 1½ cups vinegar*

**VARIATION:** Substitute 1 tablespoon of either fresh oregano, thyme, chervil, or tarragon for the basil. Or, substitute cider vinegar for the wine vinegar.

# raspberry vinegar

**1½ cups white wine vinegar**
**½ cup sugar**
**1 cup fresh raspberries or sliced strawberries, crushed**

1. Combine vinegar and sugar in nonaluminum 2-quart saucepan. Heat until very hot, stirring occasionally. Do not boil. (If vinegar boils, it will become cloudy.)

2. Pour into glass bowl; stir in raspberries. Cover with plastic wrap. Refrigerate about 1 week or until desired amount of flavor develops. Strain through fine mesh sieve or cheesecloth twice. Store in food storage jar or bottle with tight-fitting lid in refrigerator up to 6 months.

*Makes about 2 cups vinegar*

**TIP:** It's important that storage jars and glass bottles are washed with hot soapy water, then rinsed well with very hot water before use.

*herbed vinegar (left) and raspberry vinegar (right)*

# eggnog cherry quick bread mix

**1 cup all-purpose flour**
**¾ cup sugar**
**½ cup chopped candied or dried cherries**
**¾ cup chopped pecans**
**1¼ cups all-purpose flour**
**1 tablespoon baking powder**
**1 teaspoon ground nutmeg**
**½ teaspoon salt**

1. Layer all ingredients in order listed above in 1-quart food storage jar with tight-fitting lid. (Pack ingredients down lightly before adding another layer.)

2. Cover top of jar with 8-inch circle of fabric; attach recipe gift tag with raffia or ribbon. *Makes 1 (1-quart) jar*

**GIFT IDEA:** Assemble a gift basket with a jar of Eggnog Cherry Quick Bread Mix, a package of gourmet coffee or tea, and 3 miniature (5½×3-inch) loaf pans.

# eggnog cherry quick bread

**1 jar Eggnog Cherry Quick Bread Mix**
**1¼ cups prepared dairy eggnog or half-and-half**
**2 eggs**
**6 tablespoons (¾ stick) butter, melted and cooled**
**1 teaspoon vanilla**

1. Preheat oven to 350°F. Spray 3 miniature (5½×3-inch) loaf pans with nonstick cooking spray.

2. Place contents of jar into large bowl; stir until blended. Whisk together eggnog, eggs, butter, and vanilla in separate bowl. Add eggnog mixture to flour mixture; stir just until moistened. Divide equally into prepared pans.

3. Bake 35 to 40 minutes or until toothpicks inserted into centers come out clean. Cool in pans 15 minutes. Remove from pans to wire racks; cool completely. Store tightly wrapped in plastic wrap at room temperature.

*Makes 3 miniature loaves*

# rich & creamy cocoa mix

**¾ cup powdered nondairy creamer**
**½ cup nonfat dry milk powder**
**½ cup milk chocolate chips**
**¼ cup granulated sugar**
**¼ cup packed light brown sugar**
**3 tablespoons unsweetened cocoa powder**
**⅛ teaspoon salt**
**8 peppermint sticks**

1. Combine all ingredients except peppermint sticks in bowl; mix well. Place mix in 1-pint food storage jar* with tight-fitting lid. (Pack ingredients down lightly before adding another layer.) Evenly place peppermint sticks around inside of jar or tie to outside of jar with ribbon.

2. Cover top of jar with 8-inch circle of fabric; attach recipe gift tag with raffia or ribbon. *Makes 1 (1-pint) jar*

**GIFT-GIVING TIP:** Line a gift basket with decorative napkins or tea towels. Add a jar of Rich & Creamy Cocoa Mix and holiday coffee mugs. Pop in a can of refrigerated aerosol whipped cream at the last minute.

*Double the ingredients to make a one-quart jar mix.*

# rich & creamy cocoa

**1 jar Rich & Creamy Cocoa Mix**
**6 cups boiling water**
**Whipped cream**

1. Remove peppermint sticks from jar; set aside. Place cocoa mix in medium saucepan. Add water; stir until mix is dissolved and chips are melted. Keep warm over low heat.

2. Pour into individual coffee mugs. Add 1 peppermint stick to each cup; garnish with dollop of whipped cream. *Makes 8 (¾-cup) servings*

**VARIATION:** Crush peppermint sticks and add to cocoa or sprinkle over whipped cream as garnish.

**LIQUEUR-FLAVORED COCOA:** Add 1 tablespoon coffee-flavored or amaretto-flavored liqueur to each cup of cocoa. Use cinnamon sticks for stirrers.

## helpful hint

*For a single serving, place ¼ cup cocoa mix in coffee cup; add ¾ cup boiling water. Stir with peppermint stick until mix is dissolved and chocolate chips are melted. Garnish with dollop of whipped cream. If using large coffee mugs, double the recipe for the single serving.*

# santa's peppermint chocolates mix

**1 cup (6 ounces) semisweet chocolate chips**
**¼ cup white chocolate chips**
**½ cup milk chocolate chips**
**¼ cup crushed peppermint candy (about 10 peppermint candy rounds)**

1. Layer all ingredients except crushed peppermint in order listed above in 1-pint food storage jar with tight-fitting lid. (Pack ingredients down firmly before adding another layer.) Place peppermint in small plastic food storage bag. Close with twist tie; cut off top of bag. Place bag in jar.

2. Cover top of jar with 8-inch circle of fabric; attach recipe gift tag with raffia or ribbon.                                              *Makes 1 (1-pint) jar*

**TIP:** To crush candies, place candies in plastic food storage bag. Crush with rolling pin or mallet. Or, process in food processor using on/off pulsing action.

**GIFT-GIVING TIP:** Share the holiday spirit with beautifully decorated gifts. Look for inexpensive antique plates, relish trays, or vintage glassware at flea markets or antique stores. Assemble with a decorated gift jar in a holiday package. Tie with a generous bow for a simple yet spectacular gift.

## santa's peppermint chocolates

**1 jar Santa's Peppermint Chocolates Mix**

**Microwave Directions**

1. Line 8-inch square baking pan with foil; butter foil. Set aside.

2. Remove peppermint. Place remaining contents of jar in microwavable 2-cup glass measuring cup. Microwave at HIGH 1 to 2 minutes, stirring after every 30 seconds until chips are melted. Spoon chocolate into prepared pan spreading evenly over bottom to within ½ inch of sides. Sprinkle with peppermint; press into chocolate. Refrigerate until almost firm before cutting into squares. Refrigerate until firm before removing foil.                          *Makes about 3 dozen candies*

**SERVING SUGGESTION:** For a festive presentation, place individual candy pieces in paper or foil candy cups.

# rum fruitcake cookies mix

**1½ cups all-purpose flour**
**1 cup (4 ounces) chopped candied mixed fruit**
**½ cup sugar**
**½ cup nuts, coarsely chopped**
**½ cup raisins**
**1 teaspoon baking powder**
**½ teaspoon salt**
**½ teaspoon baking soda**

1. Layer ingredients attractively in any order in 1-quart food storage jar with tight-fitting lid. (Pack ingredients down firmly before adding another layer.)

2. Cover top of jar with 8-inch circle of fabric; attach recipe gift tag with raffia or ribbon.

*Makes 1 (1-quart) jar*

# rum fruitcake cookies

**⅓ cup shortening**
**2 eggs**
**3 tablespoons orange juice**
**1½ teaspoons rum extract**
**1 jar Rum Fruitcake Cookies Mix**

1. Preheat oven to 375°F. Lightly grease cookie sheets.

2. Beat shortening in large bowl until smooth. Beat in eggs, orange juice, and rum extract until blended. (Mixture may appear curdled.) Add cookie mix to shortening mixture; stir until well blended.

3. Drop rounded teaspoonfuls of dough 2 inches apart onto prepared cookie sheets. Bake 11 to 13 minutes or until golden. Do not overbake. Let cookies stand on cookie sheets 2 minutes. Remove cookies to wire racks to cool completely.

*Makes 3 dozen cookies*

## helpful hint

*Assemble a napkin-lined gift basket with a jar of Luscious Orange-Cranberry Scones Mix, oranges, and a package of premium coffee or tea. Add a nonstick silicone baking mat for the gourmet cook.*

# luscious orange-cranberry scones mix

**1 cup all-purpose flour**
**¾ cup dried cranberries or dried blueberries**
**½ cup packed brown sugar**
**¼ cup granulated sugar**
**1 cup all-purpose flour**
**2 teaspoons baking powder**
**½ teaspoon ground ginger**
**½ teaspoon ground cinnamon**
**¼ teaspoon baking soda**
**¼ teaspoon salt**
**½ cup powdered sugar**

1. Layer all ingredients except powdered sugar in order listed above in 1-quart food storage jar with tight-fitting lid. (Pack ingredients down firmly before adding another layer.) Place powdered sugar in small plastic food storage bag. Close with twist tie; cut off top of bag. Place bag in jar.

2. Cover top of jar with 8-inch circle of fabric; attach recipe gift tag with raffia or ribbon.                                                    *Makes 1 (1-quart) jar*

## helpful hint

*If jar mix contains dried blueberries, use lemon extract and lemon juice to make Luscious Lemon-Blueberry Scones.*

## luscious orange-cranberry scones

**1 jar Luscious Orange-Cranberry Scones Mix**
**6 tablespoons (¾ stick) butter, cut into pieces and softened**
**½ cup buttermilk**
**1 egg**
**2 teaspoons grated orange or lemon peel**
**1 teaspoon orange or lemon extract**
**2 to 3 teaspoons orange or lemon juice**

1. Preheat oven to 350°F. Lightly grease baking sheet.

2. Remove powdered sugar from jar. Place remaining contents of jar into large bowl. Cut in butter with pastry blender or 2 knives until mixture resembles coarse crumbs. Whisk together buttermilk, egg, orange peel, and orange extract in small bowl. Add buttermilk mixture to flour mixture. Stir until stiff dough is formed. Knead in bowl. Drop by ¼ cupfuls onto prepared baking sheet.

3. Bake 18 to 20 minutes or until toothpicks inserted into centers come out clean. Remove to wire racks; cool 10 minutes. Stir together powdered sugar and enough orange juice to make glaze. Drizzle over scones. Serve warm.

*Makes 12 scones*

*luscious orange-cranberry scones*

# cranberry-pecan muffins mix

**1¾ cups all-purpose flour**
**1 cup dried cranberries**
**¾ cup chopped pecans**
**½ cup packed light brown sugar**
**2½ teaspoons baking powder**
**½ teaspoon salt**

1. Layer ingredients attractively in any order in 1-quart food storage jar with tight-fitting lid. (Pack ingredients down lightly before adding another layer.)

2. Cover top of jar with 8-inch circle of fabric; attach recipe gift tag with raffia or ribbon. *Makes 1 (1-quart) jar*

## cranberry-pecan muffins

**1 jar Cranberry-Pecan Muffins Mix**
**¾ cup milk**
**¼ cup (½ stick) butter, melted**
**1 egg, beaten**

1. Preheat oven to 400°F. Grease or paper-line 12 standard (2½-inch) muffin pan cups.

2. Pour contents of jar into large bowl. Combine milk, butter, and egg in small bowl until blended; stir into jar mixture just until moistened. Spoon evenly into prepared muffin cups.

3. Bake 16 to 18 minutes or until toothpicks inserted into centers come out clean. Cool in pan on wire rack 5 minutes; remove from pan and cool completely on wire rack. *Makes 12 muffins*

*cranberry-pecan muffin mix*

# glorious sugared nuts mix

**½ cup whole blanched almonds, toasted\* and cooled**
**1 bar (7-ounces) milk chocolate, broken into pieces**
**1 cup whole pecans, toasted\* and cooled**
**2 tablespoons unsweetened cocoa powder**
**2 teaspoons ground cinnamon**
**½ cup powdered sugar**

*\*Place nuts in microwavable dish. Microwave at HIGH 1 to 2 minutes or just until light golden brown, stirring every 30 seconds. Let stand 3 minutes; cool completely.*

1. Layer almonds, chocolate pieces, and pecans in 1-pint food storage jar with tight-fitting lid. (Pack ingredients down firmly before adding another layer.) Place cocoa powder and cinnamon in small plastic food storage bag. Place powdered sugar in second bag. Close each bag with twist tie; cut off tops of bags. Place bags in jar.

2. Cover top of jar with 8-inch circle of fabric; attach recipe gift tag with raffia or ribbon. *Makes 1 (1-pint) jar*

**COFFEE-FLAVORED SUGARED NUTS:** Add 1 tablespoon instant espresso powder or instant coffee granules to bag of cocoa and cinnamon.

**GIFT-GIVING TIP:** For an extra touch of holiday magic, give a jar of Glorious Sugared Nuts Mix along with a sparkling glass or vintage candy dish—the perfect gift for both old and new friends.

# glorious sugared nuts

**1 jar Glorious Sugared Nuts Mix**

1. Line baking sheet with foil. Set aside.

2. Remove powdered sugar and cocoa mixture from jar. Place remaining contents of jar into medium nonstick skillet. Stir mixture over medium heat until chocolate is melted and nuts are coated with chocolate. Remove skillet from heat. Sprinkle cocoa mixture over nuts; stir to coat.

3. Place powdered sugar in medium bowl. Add nuts; stir to coat with sugar. Separate into small pieces. Spread on prepared baking sheet to cool. Store in tightly covered container. *Makes about 1½ cups nuts*

# rich chocolate sauce

**1 cup whipping cream**
**⅓ cup light corn syrup**
**1 cup (6 ounces) semisweet chocolate chips**
**1 to 2 tablespoons dark rum (optional)**
**1 teaspoon vanilla**

Place cream and corn syrup in heavy 2-quart saucepan. Stir over medium heat until mixture boils. Remove from heat. Stir in chocolate, rum, if desired, and vanilla until chocolate is melted. Cool 10 minutes. Serve warm or pour into clean glass food storage jars and seal tightly. Store up to 6 months in refrigerator. Reheat sauce over low heat before serving.                    *Makes about 1¾ cups sauce*

# pumpkin spice mini muffins mix

**2 cups all-purpose flour**
**2 teaspoons baking powder**
**¾ teaspoon salt**
**½ teaspoon baking soda**
**½ teaspoon ground ginger**
**¼ teaspoon ground nutmeg**
**¼ teaspoon ground cloves**
**¾ cup chopped dried cranberries**
**½ cup brown sugar**
**¼ cup granulated sugar**
**1 teaspoon ground cinnamon**

1. Layer all ingredients except granulated sugar and cinnamon in the order listed above in 1-quart food storage jar with tight-fitting lid. (Pack ingredients down lightly before adding another layer.) Place granulated sugar and cinnamon in small plastic food storage bag. Close with twist tie; cut off top of bag. Place bag in jar.

2. Cover top of jar with 8-inch circle of fabric; attach recipe gift tag with raffia or ribbon.                                        *Makes 1 (1-quart) jar*

# pumpkin spice mini muffins

**1 jar Pumpkin Spice Mini Muffins Mix**
**½ cup (1 stick) butter, softened**
**1 cup solid-pack pumpkin**
**2 eggs**
**½ cup orange juice**
**1 teaspoon vanilla**

1. Preheat oven to 400°F. Grease or paper-line 36 mini (1¾-inch) or 12 standard (2½-inch) muffin pan cups.

2. Remove cinnamon and sugar mixture from jar. Place remaining contents of jar in large bowl; stir until well blended. Beat butter in medium bowl with electric mixer at medium speed until creamy. Beat in pumpkin, eggs, orange juice, and vanilla until well blended. (Mixture may appear curdled.) Add to flour mixture; stir just until moistened. Spoon evenly into prepared muffin cups, filling each cup ¾ full.

3. Bake 12 to 15 minutes or until toothpicks inserted into centers come out clean. Remove muffins from pans. Place cinnamon and sugar mixture in small bowl. Roll warm muffins in sugar. Serve immediately.

*Makes about 36 miniature or 12 regular muffins*

*pumpkin spice mini muffins*

# "m&m's"® gift jar cookie mix

**¾ cup all-purpose flour**
**1 teaspoon baking soda**
**½ teaspoon salt**
**½ teaspoon ground cinnamon**
**½ cup chopped walnuts**
**1 cup "M&M's"® Chocolate Mini Baking Bits, divided**
**½ cup raisins**
**¾ cup firmly packed light brown sugar**
**1¼ cups uncooked quick oats**

In medium bowl combine flour, baking soda, salt, and cinnamon. In 1-quart clear glass jar with tight-fitting resealable lid, layer flour mixture, walnuts, ½ cup "M&M's"® Chocolate Mini Baking Bits, raisins, brown sugar, remaining ½ cup "M&M's"® Chocolate Mini Baking Bits, and oats. Seal jar; wrap decoratively. Give as a gift with the following instructions: Preheat oven to 350°F. Lightly grease cookie sheets; set aside. In large bowl beat ¾ cup (1½ sticks) butter, 1 large egg, and ¾ teaspoon vanilla extract until well blended. Stir in contents of jar until well blended. Shape into 1-inch balls and place about 2 inches apart on prepared cookie sheets. Bake 12 to 15 minutes. Cool 2 minutes on cookie sheets; cool completely on wire racks. Store in tightly covered container.

*Makes 4 dozen cookies*

*"m&m's"® gift jar cookie mix*

# sweet potato muffins mix

**2 cups flour**
**1 tablespoon baking powder**
**1 teaspoon ground cinnamon**
**½ teaspoon baking soda**
**½ teaspoon salt**
**¼ teaspoon ground nutmeg**
**½ cup packed brown sugar**
**¾ cup chopped walnuts**
**¾ cup golden raisins**

1. Combine flour, baking powder, cinnamon, baking soda, salt, and nutmeg in large bowl. Layer flour mixture, brown sugar, walnuts, and raisins in 1-quart food storage jar with tight-fitting lid. (Pack ingredients down lightly before adding each layer.)

2. Cover top of jar with 8-inch circle of fabric; attach recipe gift tag with raffia or ribbon. *Makes 1 (1-quart) jar*

## sweet potato muffins

**1 cup mashed cooked sweet potato**
**¾ cup milk**
**½ cup (1 stick) butter, melted**
**2 eggs, beaten**
**1½ teaspoons vanilla**
**1 jar Sweet Potato Muffins Mix**

1. Preheat oven to 400°F. Grease 24 standard (2½-inch) muffin pan cups. Combine sweet potato, milk, butter, eggs, and vanilla in large bowl. Stir in contents of jar just until blended.

2. Spoon batter evenly into prepared muffin cups. Bake 15 minutes or until toothpicks inserted into centers come out clean. Cool in pans 5 minutes; remove to wire racks. *Makes 2 dozen muffins*

*sweet potato muffins*

# deck the halls

**The sound of** a crackling fire. The joy of newly fallen snow. The anticipation of Santa Claus. The smell of a cedar tree. The taste of a freshly baked Christmas cookie. At its very essence, Christmas is a holiday that excites our senses. How things sound, look, feel, smell, and taste evoke memories of holidays past, flooding us with emotions. The best way to re-create these memories—and to create new memories for our families—is to surround ourselves with things that remind us of the season. Decorating is one of the easiest ways to accomplish this. Whether you are a softy for a traditional red and green Christmas or love the look of a cool blue and green holiday, decking your home in seasonal splendor will satiate the senses and fill everyone in your family with holiday spirit.

# the colors of christmas

Christmas is all about color. Glowing strings of lights, festive stockings, and beautifully wrapped gifts take center stage. The colors you choose to emphasize in your holiday decorations can impact the feelings they evoke. Consider your goals—icy and intense, cozy and traditional, modern and fresh, elegant and luxurious—before deciding on a color scheme.

## "i'll have a blue christmas..."

Cool blue looks icy and cold, like the light of winter after a heavy snow has settled. The spectrum ranges from pale blue so light it shimmers to shocking cobalt. Whether you choose to use various shades all together or stick with one main color, blue will electrify and intensify your decorating scheme. White or silver is often added to enhance the décor; mixing in greenery and other naturals can also accentuate the various hues of blue.

*Silver and blue create a cool presentation. Pink silk camellias tucked between tree branches accentuate the glitter of the balls.*

# softly silver wreath

THIS WREATH GLISTENS WITH
HUES OF SILVER AND BLUE,
WHILE THE FLUFFY FEATHERS ARE
A REMINDER OF FRESHLY
FALLEN SNOW.

## what you'll need

14-inch white foam wreath
6 yards white feather boa
Floral U pins
Assorted evergreen sprigs
Wire cutters
Hot glue gun, glue sticks
3½ yards silver metallic ribbon,
    1½ inches wide
Scissors
Floral wire

4 yards blue metallic wire
Iridescent tissue paper
Ruler
5 floral picks, 2 inches each
Ivy leaves
Silver foliage sprays
Christmas balls, assorted sizes:
    silver, clear, blue
Chenille stem

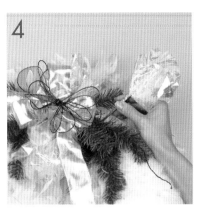

1 Starting on outside edge, pin feather boa around wreath with U pins. Continue around wreath, pinning boa to middle-top of wreath. Don't worry about covering the inside edge; feathers will cover foam.

2 Cut evergreen sprigs into small lengths with wire cutters. Use U pins to place them across top of wreath in an arc. Hot glue to secure.

3 Form silver ribbon into a 6-loop bow with 3-inch loops and 12-inch streamers; secure with floral wire. Glue bow to top center of wreath in middle of evergreens. Place steamers so they cascade down sides of wreath. Trim ribbon ends on a diagonal.

4 Form blue wire into a multi-loop bow; secure in center with floral wire. Insert and glue blue bow on top of silver bow. Cut five 4-inch squares from tissue paper. Form each into a puff, and attach to a floral pick. Insert tissue squares around bows.

5 Glue in ivy leaves as shown. Insert and glue silver foliage cascading down the right and left sides of wreath. Using photo as a guide, glue in silver, clear, and blue Christmas balls.

6 Twist chenille stem into a loop, and insert it into top back of wreath for a hanger. Secure loop with floral U pins. Glue in place.

# holiday pear garland

THE GREENS IN THIS PEAR GARLAND MAKE A PERFECT ACCENT TO A COOL BLUE HOLIDAY DECORATING SCHEME. PLACE IT OVER A DOORWAY, LET IT CASCADE DOWN A STAIRCASE, OR USE IT TO ADORN A TABLE.

## what you'll need

Stem floral wire, 22 gauge
Wire cutters
Ruler
36 faux pears
Brown floral tape
8 green berry stems
5 silk lemon leaf stems
2 pine sprays with gold glitter
Natural birch branches
9-foot silk pine garland
2 gold holly sprays
Hot glue gun, glue sticks

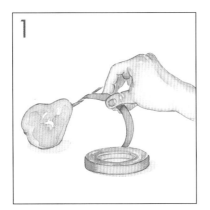

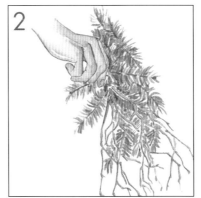

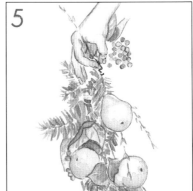

1 Cut the floral wire into 6-inch lengths. Extend stem ends of pears with floral wire by covering wire and stem with brown floral tape. Set aside. Cut berry stems, lemon leaf stems, and pine sprays into 4- to 5-inch pieces. Set aside.

2 Place birch branches in pine garland, and twist pine branches around birch to hold in place. Use floral wire if needed for extra security. Birch branches should extend 4 to 5 inches from pine garland.

3 Use floral wire to add berry stems, pine sprays, and lemon leaf stems to garland.

4 Add pears by twisting stem ends into garland. Add extra branches, berries, and other leaves as needed to give garland a full and lush look.

5 Cut holly sprays into small pieces, and glue into garland. Use them to hide any wire that shows.

 variations

*For a novel approach, add feathered partridges to remind guests of the 12 days of Christmas. Tuck in ribbons or small bows for added texture and color. Make place cards to coordinate a party theme. Cut a small slit into the top of a faux pear, and tuck in a small card with a guest's name on it. Make one for each dinner guest!*

*All it takes to pull off a themed holiday is a bit of planning. Choose a color scheme and apply it to ornaments, tablescapes, wrapping paper, and ribbons to make your décor come alive.*

work well together because they are opposite each other on the color wheel. In practice, red and green go together in almost any setting in your home, from a mantel festooned with a natural garland and flanked with red stockings to a table centerpiece that highlights Christmas china.

## seeing red—and green

Conjure up memories of Christmas past, and you likely envision a holiday decked out in red and green. These colors are synonymous with Christmas; they're the traditional colors most often associated with the season. Technically, red and green

*What says Christmas better than red paired with green? For a rich, refined display, generously group the same ornaments or materials for impact.*

# lush and lovely lodge wreath

BEAUTIFULLY TEXTURED EVERGREENS, BRIGHT RED BERRIES, AND A BOLD RIBBON MAKE THIS CHARMING WREATH A HOLIDAY FAVORITE. IT ADDS A SWEETLY NOSTALGIC TOUCH TO A RED AND GREEN CHRISTMAS.

## what you'll need

20-inch artificial evergreen wreath of mixed greens
2 black chenille stems
1½ yards red-and-black plaid ribbon, 2½ inches wide
Hot glue gun, glue sticks
10 pinecones
6 dried pomegranates
Heavy-duty scissors or wire cutters
Assorted foliage
Berry clusters: 4 burgundy, 4 red
2 red berry sprays, 12 inches each

3

5

1 Shape wreath to increase fullness and achieve a natural look. To make hanger, twist a chenille stem into loop on top back of wreath.

2 About 12 inches from one end of ribbon, form two 6-inch loops. Pinch loops together, and secure with chenille stem to form bow.

3 Glue bow to upper left side of wreath. Weave bow's streamers into wreath, and glue in place. Glue pinecones in wreath as shown.

4 Cut pomegranate stems to 1 inch, and glue 2 pomegranates in center of bow. Glue remaining pomegranates in clusters of 2, equally spaced around wreath.

5 Cut foliage into short lengths, and glue between pinecones and pomegranates. Glue a few sprigs over top of bow.

6 Glue burgundy berry clusters equally spaced around wreath; repeat with red berry clusters. Cut red berry sprays into 4-inch lengths, and glue into wreath as desired.

 tip

*When working on a wreath or other floral arrangement that is designed to hang, you may want to work with it in a hanging position to get the right perspective.*

 tip

*If you can't find a ribbon you like, cut 3-inch-wide fabric strips, and turn and glue the edges under slightly. Then form a bow as you would with a ribbon.*

# christmas arch

ADD A TOUCH OF RED AND GREEN TO A FOYER OR DOORWAY WITH THIS ELEGANT FLORAL ARCH. PINE WAS USED AS A BACKGROUND, WHILE A GLITTERING TAPESTRY BOW, BRANCHES OF RED BERRIES, AND STEMS OF CINNAMON STICKS ADD THE FINISHING TOUCHES.

## what you'll need

30-inch artificial Christmas wreath
3 yards ribbon (3 inches wide)
Stem floral wire, 22 gauge
8 berry sprays
Brown floral tape
Hot glue gun, glue sticks
14 to 16 cinnamon sticks
18 small to medium pinecones
Wire cutters

1

3

4

2

3 Fluff the branches of the arch. Use wires to attach bow to the center of the arch. If berry sprays are not long enough, wrap floral tape around the end of the spray and attach a length of stem wire. Glue cinnamon sticks, berry sprays, and pinecones jutting out from each side of the bow.

4 Taper the ends of the arch by snipping off sprigs with wire cutters. To attach hanger, cover stem wire with brown floral tape. Twist the wire around the middle of the heavy wire of the wreath in the back and twist to make a loop.

1 Bend the wreath in half.

2 Combine the two halves to make an arch by twisting pieces of the wired greens together. Make a two-loop bow by measuring the desired tail length from the end of your ribbon and making a loop on each side of your thumb. Twist stem wire around center of bow to hold shape; bring wire to back.

*For a subtle atmosphere, go all-white with hints of naturals and greenery for contrast throughout the room.*

## "i'm dreaming of a white christmas"

A white Christmas can be classic and traditional or glamorous and fresh. That's the beauty of decorating with such a versatile color. With contemporary interiors, an all-white Christmas is en vogue: current, up-to-date, modern. With traditional décors, all white lends a homespun feel to the holidays. Twinkling white lights and touches of silver are spectacular accents to an all-white decorating scheme. Flickering candles or a roaring fire add warmth to pure white and play up the shimmery effect of any gold or silver accents.

# southern magnolia holiday wreath

THE SOUTH'S MOST BEAUTIFUL FLOWER IS HIGHLIGHTED IN THIS FORMAL HOLIDAY WREATH. ELEGANT IVORY MAGNOLIAS DANCE THROUGH CHRISTMAS GREENERY, GLASS ORNAMENTS, AND GOLDEN HOLLY LEAVES.

## what you'll need

5 silk magnolias
4 silk magnolia buds
Wire cutters
Floral wire
Artificial pine wreath
Hot glue gun, glue sticks
27 one-inch gold glass ball ornaments on wire picks
Tape measure
2 gold silk holly branches
72 inches sheer wired ribbon
10 natural pinecones

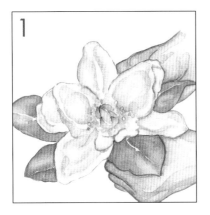

1 Cut stems of magnolia flowers to 2 inches. Cut off buds and leaves from stems. Form a collar around flower with discarded magnolia leaves, and wrap with floral wire to hold in place. Do the same with buds.

2 Insert magnolias and buds into wreath, spacing evenly to leave room for ornaments. Twist pine branches around stems to secure. Add a touch of hot glue for extra security.

3 Twist 3 glass balls together to form a cluster. Make 9 clusters. Insert clusters into wreath between magnolias. Twist pine branches around clusters to hold them in place.

4 Cut holly branches into 3- to 4-inch pieces. Glue them into wreath around magnolias. Glue remaining magnolia leaves to hide any wire.

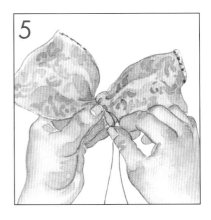

5 Cut ribbon into three 24-inch pieces. Form 2 loops of ribbon, and twist together with floral wire. Secure each ribbon to wreath behind a magnolia. Keep ribbon loops to sides of flowers so flowers remain dominant. Space ribbons evenly around wreath.

6 Glue in pinecones and remaining holly leaves to hide any glue or wire.

### try this!

*The gold and ivory color combination of this wreath can be changed to suit your home décor. Consider using red, green, or even blue ornaments to complement the classic ivory magnolias. Red and green trim would give the wreath a more traditional appeal for the Christmas season.*

# shimmering snowflake wreath

THIS SPECTACULAR WREATH
IS INSPIRED BY IMAGES OF
DELICATE SNOWFLAKES.
THE GOLD TOUCHES ADD
A BIT OF SPARKLE TO
THE CRISP WHITES.

## what you'll need

20 pinecones on picks, 2 inches each
Gold metallic spray
Hot glue gun, glue sticks
20-inch pine wreath
5 yards white/gold sheer wired ribbon with gold stars, 3 inches wide
Ruler
Scissors
Cloth-covered wire
Wire cutters
10 plastic frosted snowflakes, 4 inches each
84 inches gold metallic tubing, ⅜ inches wide

1 Spray pinecones with gold spray. Let dry. Apply glue to each pinecone and position throughout wreath.

2 Form 8-loop bow with the sheer wired ribbon. Each should measure 3½ inches. Cut off remaining ribbon. Use cloth-covered wire to secure bow. Wire the bow onto the wreath, securing with extra wire.

3 Drape remaining ribbon around wreath, using wired pine branches to wrap around ribbon and hold in place.

4 Apply a small amount of glue to tip of each snowflake and place around wreath.

5 Cut metallic tubing into 12-inch lengths. Form 2 loops with each length and secure with cloth-covered wire. Trim excess wire. Glue these throughout design.

*Gilded vegetables and fruits make striking holiday embellishments. Here, a pumpkin festooned in silver leaf adds a unique touch to a silver decorating scheme.*

## silver and gold, silver and gold

Make a splashy statement by decorating with silver and gold. These rich metallics have an elegant, luxurious appeal, especially when used together or in conjunction with one other color. If backing away from traditional red and green seems daunting, add ornaments and decorations in silver and gold piece by piece for a few seasons before going all out with this dramatic color scheme.

# candy-coated christmas

You will have visions of sugarplums dancing in your head when you make this sparkling holiday wreath. Assorted miniature fruit, berries, and mint candy canes glisten with a "candy coating" of diamond dust. This evergreen wreath will bring out the child in all of us.

## what you'll need

Small artist's paintbrush
54 pieces artificial fruit on wire picks
White craft glue
Diamond dust or opalescent glitter
2 stems red berries
2 dozen plastic candy canes
Artificial pine wreath, 14 inches
Hot glue gun, glue sticks

1

3

4

1 Using small artist's paintbrush, coat each piece of fruit with glue. Sprinkle diamond dust over fruit pieces. Repeat process on berries and candy canes. Let dry overnight.

2 Shape evergreen wreath by pulling out and fluffing branches.

3 Twist 3 pieces of different fruit together into a cluster. Place fruit clusters into wreath. Twist stems of fruit into branches. Continue around wreath until it is full.

5

4 Cut each berry stem into 5 or so pieces; each piece should have about 5 berries. Glue berry stems into wreath. Spread berries throughout wreath.

5 Glue candy canes into wreath at an angle so that they stick out from fruits and berries.

 variation

*For a variation, add a bow to this sparkling confection. Choose a soft color for the ribbon so you don't detract from the pastels of the fruit. Attach a small bow with streamers to the bottom of the wreath for a more elegant look.*

# decorating sensations

When you think of decorating for the holidays, you probably imagine a lush tree, twinkling lights, and dangling stockings. But don't forget your table and mantel! A beautiful table makes delicious meals all the more decadent, and an elegant mantel makes those crackling fires all the brighter.

## quick and easy centerpieces

A centerpiece doesn't have to be showy to be sensational. A small Christmas tree topped with a silver star is an elegant touch for an inti-

*Metallic beads, glass ornaments, and sheer ribbon give a wrought-iron chandelier an easy face-lift for the holidays. Such an unexpected touch is bound to create a stir.*

*Centerpieces add panache to a tablescape. These stylized vases of roses and berries are a well-appointed decoration for an all-red table setting.*

mate family affair. On the other hand, going all out with a bedecked arrangement is bound to impress dinner guests. Keep in mind that the best centerpieces blossom above or spread out below the sight line, enabling guests to make eye contact during conversation. If you use candles, position them out of the way of plates and glasses.

# holiday dinner party

## what you'll need

Dry floral foam
Knife
4- to 6-inch-high brass bowl
Hot glue gun, glue sticks
Ruler
Evergreen bough
14 Christmas ornament balls
12 small pinecones
1 spray of plums (or about 7 plums)
4 berry sprays, cut into pieces
3 poinsettia flowers with leaves

## centerpiece

1 Cut floral foam to fit the bowl; glue. (Use a plastic liner if you don't want to glue bowl.) Cut bough into five- to six-inch lengths. Form width and length by gluing greens around edge of container.

2 Mound Christmas ornaments, pinecones, plums, and berry sprays on the greens and floral foam and secure with hot glue.

3 Glue sprigs of greens, poinsettia flowers, and other poinsettia leaves to fill in holes between ornaments and pinecones.

## place card holders

Cut pieces, two- to three-inch lengths, from bough. Glue sprigs of greens and a few berries to base of ornament, making sure ornament stands upright.

*It doesn't take much to transform your mantel. Greenery, Christmas balls, and luxurious ribbon are quick and easy ingredients for elegance.*

spray-painting them with metallic chrome paint. Pot poinsettias in each, and space evenly across your mantel. Fill in the gaps with bits of greenery.

Create a natural scene by bringing the outdoors inside. Gather sturdy sticks, pinecones, magnolia cones, and large leaves from your yard. Rub with gilding rub, wiping off excess as needed. Tack the leaves together to create a garland that is twice as long as your mantel. Arrange the items on top of the mantel, draping the leaf garland over and around so that it falls naturally off the mantel in places. For color, place candles in an assortment of sizes and shapes on pedestals throughout the arrangement and tuck pieces of thick-skin fruit such as lemons, limes, and oranges into the foliage.

For a more traditional look, purchase several small artificial Christmas trees and wrap the bases with colorful holiday fabric. Checked taffeta, a rich damask, delicate lace, even quilt batting can be used with success. Decorate the trees with tiny Christmas balls and ornaments or leave them bare and top with a single gold or silver star.

## dress your mantel for the holidays

Already the focal point in the room, the mantel is an excellent starting point for your holiday decorating. Treasured heirlooms, holiday cards, and stocking holders are a given when it comes to decorating the mantel. But why not spice it up a little this year?

Pretty up poinsettias by buying six terra-cotta pots and saucers and

# christmas mantel topper

ADD ELEGANCE AND CHARM TO YOUR FIREPLACE MANTEL WITH THIS LUXURIOUS TOPPER. THERE'S NOTHING LIKE A TOUCH OF GOLD TO MAKE A ROOM SPARKLE!

## what you'll need

4 plastic oranges

3 plastic peaches

2 plastic bananas

4 plastic grape clusters

10 pinecones

Gold spray paint

4 to 6 pieces Christmas greens (mixed)

Hot glue gun, glue sticks

Pinecones

4 gold mixed holly/berry sprays

10 plastic gold ornaments

3 yards gold ribbon, 1½ inches wide

25 feet gold-star garland

1 Spray fruit and pinecones gold. While paint is drying, place greens on mantel to assemble. You will be making two sections, one for each side of the mantel. If greens are artificial, connect by twisting stems together. If greens are real, use spool wire. One side of mantelpiece should hang long, with the other side shorter but thicker.

2 Once you have both sides assembled, take the greens back to your craft table to finish. Mound the gold fruit and glue pieces to the greens. Glue pinecones, berry sprays, and gold ornaments to add different shapes and textures into your design.

3 Entwine ribbon among greens. Unwind gold-star garland and loosely attach to the greens.

# elegant entertaining

**A successful party** lives on in everyone's memory long after the last glass of punch has been sipped and the last bite of dessert eaten. But the fuss and frustration of planning can be a big party pooper. All the details—*What kind of party should I have? Whom should I invite? How should I decorate? What do I serve?*—can make even the most experienced host or hostess a little stressed. That's why we've included lots of party themes, ideas, and menus that make it easy to pull off a spectacular event. Our tried-and-true secrets for entertaining will ensure that your party is one to remember!

# party planning with panache

Any event planner or caterer will tell you the key to a successful party is planning. It's not enough to simply make a few dishes and send invitations. A little advance planning saves you time and headaches later so spend five or ten minutes envisioning the party and walking yourself through as a guest. When party time comes, both you and your guests will have a night to remember!

## dreaming of the perfect party

The holiday season is packed with parties, so it's a good idea to send invitations three weeks in advance. The sooner you send your invitations, the less likely it is that your guests will have committed to another event. Your invitations should state the starting and ending time of your party and should mention the food you will be serving, whether it is light holiday fare or a traditional sit-down dinner. And don't forget to include directions!

Choose a menu for which many of the items can be made ahead of time. Some appetizers and desserts can be made and frozen several weeks in advance. Other recipes can be mixed together a few days before and stored in the refrigerator. Simply bake and finish the day of the party. Remember that parties aren't the time to try a new recipe. Either test a new menu item before the party, or stick with tried-and-true recipes.

Opt for heavy finger foods instead of recipes that require dinnerware. Foods that can be eaten without a fork and knife keep spills and dribbles down, and they reduce the amount of dishwashing you have to do later. If you do serve dishes that require dinnerware, make sure you have table seating for guests to sit down and eat. Make it easy on yourself. If you dread cleanup, opt for nice plasticware that can be tossed in the trash.

Think about traffic flow. Place your bar close to ice and water. Place trays of finger foods on side tables and buffets throughout your entertaining area. Provide enough chairs so that at least half of your guests can be seated at a time. Position several trash cans inconspicuously near the food tables and bar to prevent precarious pileups of plates and traffic jams in the kitchen.

If you don't have time to deep clean your home the day of the party, hit the heavy traffic areas such as your living room, dining room, and bathrooms, and leave the rest for later.

Set the mood with holiday music playing in the background and lit candles sparkling throughout the house. Personalize the night with a special activity. Invite your guests to write a holiday wish in a guest book displayed on your coffee table or ask them to join you for some caroling.

Little details such as these help make your party an event to remember.

Guests love party favors. Send yours home with a little something extra: a small ornament, a bag of cookies, even a candy cane with a bow is a sweet way to say happy holidays.

*English crackers are little paper party favors your guests will love. Make the crackers yourself from decorative gift wrap and ribbon, or purchase them at a party store and fill with special goodies.*

## *perfect party favors*

What better way for guests to remember your party than to send them home with a small gift? Party favors don't have to be expensive; on the contrary, the best favors are creative and thoughtful. Here are some ideas for party favors that can be used with the holiday parties discussed later in this chapter.

**English Crackers.** These small, paper favors are pulled at the ends to make the "present" inside pop out. Fill with candy, confetti, or a poem written on nice paper.

**Small Picture Frames.** Frame a seasonal image or a photo of the guest, and use it as a place card on your table. After the party, send it home with your guest as a token of the evening.

**Flowering Bulbs.** Place two or three bulbs in tulle, tie with a bow, and add planting instructions.

**Mexican Maracas.** Tie bows around small maracas and hand them out to guests as they arrive.

**Swedish-Inspired Votives.** St. Lucia Day is all about light. To commemorate, tie a ribbon around a fragrant votive and attach a personal note.

**Cute Magnets.** A holiday magnet is a year-round reminder of good times and good friends. Wrap in colored tissue paper and tie closed with a pretty bow.

**Old-World Snow Globes.** Germany is blanketed with snow during the holidays. To remember an old-world gathering, place tiny snow globes at each place setting, or line them up on your coffee table or mantel for guests to take home.

**Quotable Notes.** Create inexpensive custom notepads by printing your favorite holiday or friendship quotes onto plain paper that has been sectioned four ways so that you have four notes to one sheet. Take the paper to a local quick print store, have multiple copies made, then have them backed with cardboard and glued together along the top edges.

**French Crèches.** Purchase small nativity scenes for your Le Reveillon celebration, and write a small note of thanks on the bottom.

**Pretty Ornaments.** Wrap a pretty ornament in tissue paper, and give one to each guest as they say good night.

## inspired invitations

An invitation is your guest's first impression of what your party will be like. To build the excitement, don't settle for a phone call or purchased invitation. Instead, use your party's theme to inspire your own quirky creations.

For a nice personal touch, use a photo from last year's party as the front of your invitation, or send one with your family dressed in holiday garb or outfits that complement your party's theme. You might also have your child draw a picture of the nativity scene, your party, or a present. Scan the photo onto a computer and print onto cardstock.

Get guests into party mode by making a custom CD of holiday music or other music that goes with your party theme. Write the party details on the CD label and send in a bubble-wrap envelope.

If you'd like an invitation with a hand-crafted look, purchase holiday stamps, and use them to make custom invitations. Stamps are available in a variety of seasonal motifs, making them ideal for expressing a particular party theme.

No time to make your invitations? Purchase nice note cards, and write a handwritten invitation with black ink. This is an elegant and personal way to announce your party.

## it's party time!

The date has finally arrived. Guests will be arriving on your doorstep in minutes! You've prepared as much as possible ahead of time to ensure your plans run smoothly. A few finishing details should be all you need to make the event memorable.

Anticipate the comfort of your guests. Set appetizers in the living room, on the buffet, and in other places that make it easy to nibble. Play music and light candles for ambience.

Take guests' belongings when they arrive. Introduce people by pointing out what they have in common with each other. Accept any gifts graciously and take to a discreet place so that other guests won't feel guilty if they didn't bring one.

Finally, stay out of the kitchen as much as possible so you can mingle with your guests and enjoy the party.

# holiday menus

## christmas brunch

Evening parties are fun, but because everyone is so busy during the holidays, they can often become obligations. Instead of competing for a date, host a Christmas brunch on a weekend day before Christmas and invite friends and family to drop by as a respite from holiday shopping and other activities. This type of party is actually easy to pull off: Simply choose dishes that can be made ahead or prepared by using ready-made ingredients.

### *Menu*

Cherry Eggnog Quick Bread, page 290

Donut Spice Cakes, page 280

Fresh Cranberry Salad, page 208

Fancy Swiss Omelet Roll, page 172

Holiday Baked Ham, page 162

Mulled Cranberry Tea, page 252

## holiday dinner

Whether your family Christmas dinner is a casual or formal affair, you can count on good food and good times. These tasty recipes are a lovely complement to warm conversation and company.

### *Menu*

Crown Roast of Pork with Peach Stuffing, page 156

Asparagus Wreath, page 204

Sour Cream Garlic Mashed Potatoes, page 208

Hot Spiced Tea, page 268

Cranberry-Lime Squares, page 226

Chocolate Mint Truffles, page 294

## appetizer party swap

Similar to the cookie party swap, this get-together sends guests home with a variety of tasty appetizers for the holidays. Ask friends to make six batches of one of the recipes listed below (they can also choose a favorite recipe of their own). Dishes should be non-perishable and last from one to three weeks. Each batch should have a recipe card attached. Serve one appetizer at the party, and pack the others for guests to carry home and serve at a later date. All you need to supply are drinks and packaging such as food boxes, aluminum foil, and resealable bags.

### *Menu*

Cranberry-Orange Snack Mix, page 126

Gingerbread Caramel Corn, page 142

Hot Pepper Cranberry Jelly Appetizer, page 130

Lemon Dill Seafood Spread, page 145

Nicole's Cheddar Crisps, page 137

Roasted Sweet Pepper Tapas, page 140

## *progressive christmas caroling party*

Fa-la-la-la-la your way out of the kitchen and into the mix with a progressive Christmas caroling party. The premise is the same as that of a traditional progressive party, with a bit of caroling thrown in between: begin at one home for the first course, move on to the next for the second, and continue progressing the party to other houses for the third and following courses. You can have as many stops as you would like, but remember to have nibbles and warm drinks available at each stop.

### Menu

*1ST STOP*

Festive Nachos, page 130

Guacamole Ring, page 132

Shrimp Toast, page 154

Bacon Cheese Spread, page 138

Warming Winter Punch, page 269

Hot Buttered Cider, page 264

*2ND STOP*

Turkey-Tomato Soup, page 200

Spicy Pumpkin Soup with Green Chili Swirl, page 188

Butternut Bisque, page 202

Polenta Triangles, page 193

Holiday Appetizer Puffs, page 132

Viennese Coffee, page 248

*3RD STOP*

Little Christmas Pizzas, page 131

Sweet Jalapeño Mustard Turkey Thighs, page 170

Christmas Cabbage Slaw, page 201

Festive Cranberry Mold, page 190

Smooth Mocha Coffee, page 266

*4TH STOP*

Holiday Mini Kisses Treasure Cookies, page 228

Refrigerator Cookies, page 240

Holiday Mulled Cider, page 258

Spiced Tea (Russian-Style), page 263

Merry, Merry Christmas Cake, page 282

Merri-Mint Truffles, page 286

# feliz navidad

Mexicans celebrate the nativity and birth of Jesus with the *Posadas,* the nine days of preparation where the story of the nativity is reenacted. These days lead up to *Noche Buena,* or Holy Night of Christmas Eve. Most families go to mass, then head home for dinner with family and friends. The highlight of the evening is placing baby Jesus in the manger in the nativity scene.

Decorate your Mexican fiesta with pottery; bowls of fruit; brightly colored paper ornaments; colorful confetti; tinsel-trimmed maracas; small lanterns and candles; star piñatas filled with peanuts, oranges, tangerines, and sugar canes; red, green, and silver tablecloths; and of course, a nativity scene.

## mexican coffee

**6 cups hot brewed coffee**
**1 (14-ounce) can EAGLE BRAND® Sweetened Condensed Milk**
  **(NOT evaporated milk)**
**½ cup coffee liqueur**
**2 teaspoons vanilla extract**
**⅓ cup tequila (optional)**
  **Ground cinnamon (optional)**

1. In medium saucepan over medium heat, combine coffee, EAGLE BRAND®, and liqueur. Heat through, stirring constantly. Remove from heat; stir in vanilla and tequila, if desired.

2. Sprinkle each serving with cinnamon, if desired. Store leftovers covered in refrigerator.                                                               *Makes 8 cups*

# chilies rellenos

**Tomato Sauce (page 110)**
**8 fresh poblano or Anaheim chilies**
**Picadillo Filling (page 110)**
**Vegetable oil**
⅓ **cup all-purpose flour**
 **5 eggs, separated**
¼ **teaspoon** *each* **cream of tartar and salt**
**Pimiento-stuffed green olives for garnish (optional)**

1. Prepare Tomato Sauce.

2. Roast, peel, seed, and devein chilies, leaving stems intact and taking care not to break chilies.

3. Prepare Picadillo Filling. Carefully spoon about ¼ cup of filling into each chili; press chilies firmly between hands to ease out air and to close.

4. Heat 1 inch oil in deep, heavy skillet over medium-high heat to 375°F; adjust heat to maintain temperature. Pour flour into medium bowl. Roll each chili in flour to coat lightly; pat off excess. Reserve remaining flour, about ¼ cup.

5. Beat egg whites, cream of tartar, and salt in large bowl with electric mixer at high speed until soft peaks form. Beat egg yolks in medium bowl with electric mixer at medium speed until thick and lemon colored. Gradually beat reserved flour into egg yolks until smooth. Fold ¼ of egg whites into yolk mixture; fold in remaining egg whites until blended.

6. Line baking sheet with paper towels; reheat sauce over medium heat. Coat each chili with egg batter by grasping stems and supporting bottom of chili with fork. Dip into batter to coat; let excess drain off. Immediately place chili into oil. Fry 4 minutes or until deep gold, turning once. Remove with slotted spatula; drain on paper towels.

7. Spoon sauce on plates; arrange chilies on top of sauce. Garnish, if desired.

*Makes 4 servings*

*continued on page 110*

*chilies rellenos,* continued

## tomato sauce

**1½ pounds tomatoes, peeled and seeded**
**1 medium white onion, chopped**
**1 clove garlic, chopped**
**2 tablespoons vegetable oil**
**1½ cups chicken broth**
**½ teaspoon dried thyme leaves, crushed**
**¼ teaspoon salt**

1. Place tomatoes, onion, and garlic in blender; process until smooth. Heat oil in large skillet over medium heat until hot. Add tomato mixture; cook and stir 5 minutes.

2. Stir broth, thyme, and salt into skillet. Bring to a boil over high heat. Reduce heat to medium-low. Cook and stir 10 to 15 minutes until sauce has thickened slightly. Remove from heat; set aside.                    *Makes about 2 cups*

## picadillo filling

**1 tablespoon vegetable oil**
**¼ cup slivered almonds**
**¾ pound ground beef**
**¼ cup finely chopped white onion**
**1 large tomato, peeled, seeded, and finely chopped**
**1 tablespoon tomato paste**
**1 clove garlic, minced**
**2 tablespoons raisins**
**2 tablespoons thinly sliced pimiento-stuffed green olives**
**1 tablespoon cider vinegar**
**1 teaspoon dark brown sugar**
**¼ teaspoon *each* salt and ground cinnamon**
**⅛ teaspoon *each* ground cumin and ground cloves**

1. Heat oil in large skillet over medium heat. Add almonds; cook and stir 2 to 3 minutes or until golden. Remove; drain on paper towels.

2. Crumble beef into skillet; brown 5 minutes, stirring often. Add onion; cook and stir 4 minutes or until softened. Add tomato, tomato paste, and garlic. Cook and stir 2 minutes. Stir in remaining ingredients. Cover; simmer over low heat 15 minutes. Uncover; cook over medium-low heat 3 minutes or until liquid has evaporated. Skim and discard fat. Stir in almonds. Let stand until cool.          *Makes about 2 cups*

# st. lucia day

St. Lucia Day, or the Festival of Lights, is celebrated throughout Sweden on December 13.

Blue and white are the main colors of the celebration. White dinnerware with blue napkins is always appropriate, but you can also embellish the table with white candles, greenery, and ornaments on blue velvet ribbon hanging from the chandelier.

## roasted garlic swedish meatballs

- **1 pound ground beef**
- **½ cup plain dry bread crumbs**
- **1 egg**
- **1 jar (1 pound) RAGÚ® Cheese Creations!® Roasted Garlic Parmesan Sauce**
- **1¼ cups beef broth**
- **2 teaspoons Worcestershire sauce**
- **1 teaspoon ground allspice (optional)**

In large bowl, combine ground beef, bread crumbs, and egg; shape into 20 (1½-inch) meatballs.

In 12-inch nonstick skillet, brown meatballs over medium-high heat.

Meanwhile, in medium bowl, combine Sauce, beef broth, Worcestershire sauce, and allspice, if desired; stir into skillet. Bring to a boil over high heat. Reduce heat to low and simmer uncovered, stirring occasionally, 10 minutes or until meatballs are done and sauce is slightly thickened. Serve, if desired, over hot cooked noodles or rice.

*Makes 4 servings*

# baked ham with sweet and spicy glaze

**1 (8-pound) bone-in smoked half ham**
**Sweet and Spicy Glaze (recipe follows)**

1. Preheat oven to 325°F. Place ham, fat side up, on rack in roasting pan. Insert meat thermometer into thickest part of ham away from fat or bone. Roast ham in oven about 3 hours.

2. Prepare Sweet and Spicy Glaze. Remove ham from oven. Generously brush half of glaze over ham; return to oven 30 minutes longer or until meat thermometer registers 160°F. Remove ham from oven and brush with remaining glaze. Let ham stand about 20 minutes before slicing.          *Makes 8 to 10 servings*

## sweet and spicy glaze

**¾ cup packed brown sugar**
**⅓ cup cider vinegar**
**¼ cup golden raisins**
**1 can (8¾ ounces) sliced peaches in heavy syrup, drained, chopped and syrup reserved**
**1 tablespoon cornstarch**
**¼ cup orange juice**
**1 can (8¼ ounces) crushed pineapple in syrup, undrained**
**1 tablespoon grated orange peel**
**1 clove garlic, crushed**
**½ teaspoon red pepper flakes**
**½ teaspoon grated fresh ginger**

Combine brown sugar, vinegar, raisins, and peach syrup in medium saucepan. Bring to a boil over high heat; reduce to low and simmer 8 to 10 minutes. In small bowl, dissolve cornstarch in orange juice; add to brown sugar mixture. Add remaining ingredients; mix well. Cook over medium heat, stirring constantly, until mixture boils and thickens. Remove from heat.          *Makes about 2 cups*

# swedish limpa bread

**1¾ to 2 cups all-purpose flour, divided**
**½ cup rye flour**
**1 package (¼ ounce) active dry yeast**
**1 tablespoon sugar**
**1½ teaspoons grated orange peel**
**1 teaspoon salt**
**½ teaspoon fennel seeds, crushed**
**½ teaspoon caraway seeds, crushed**
**¾ cup plus 4 teaspoons water, divided**
**4 tablespoons molasses, divided**
**2 tablespoons margarine or butter**
**1 teaspoon instant coffee granules**
**¼ teaspoon whole fennel seeds**
**¼ teaspoon whole caraway seeds**

1. Combine 1½ cups all-purpose flour, rye flour, yeast, sugar, orange peel, salt, and crushed seeds in large bowl. Heat ¾ cup water, 3 tablespoons molasses, and margarine in small saucepan over low heat until temperature reaches 120° to 130°F. Stir in coffee. Stir water mixture into flour mixture with rubber spatula to form soft but sticky dough. Gradually add more all-purpose flour to form rough dough.

2. Turn out dough onto lightly floured surface. Knead 2 minutes or until soft dough forms, gradually adding remaining all-purpose flour to prevent sticking, if necessary. Cover with inverted bowl; let rest 5 minutes. Continue kneading 5 to 8 minutes or until smooth and elastic. Shape dough into ball; place in large greased bowl. Turn dough over so top is greased. Loosely cover with lightly greased sheet of plastic wrap. Let rise in warm place 75 minutes or until almost doubled in bulk.

3. Punch down dough. Grease 8½×4½-inch loaf pan. Roll dough into 12×7-inch rectangle. Starting with one short end, roll up tightly, jelly-roll style. Pinch seams and ends to seal. Place seam-side down in prepared pan. Cover loosely with plastic wrap. Let rise in warm place 1 hour or until doubled in bulk.

4. Preheat oven to 350°F. Stir remaining 1 tablespoon molasses and 4 teaspoons water in small bowl; set aside. Uncover loaf; make 3 diagonal slashes on top of dough using sharp knife. Bake 40 to 45 minutes or until loaf sounds hollow when tapped. Brush top with molasses mixture and sprinkle with whole fennel and caraway seeds halfway through baking time. Brush again with molasses mixture about 10 minutes before removing loaf from oven. Cool in pan on wire rack 5 minutes. Remove from pan. Cool completely on wire rack.          *Makes 12 servings*

# boxing day

In merry old England, servants were required to work on Christmas Day. However, they were given reprieve the day after to visit family. Their employers would send them off with a box containing gifts and food, hence the holiday "Boxing Day." Today, people continue to celebrate by taking the day off to visit family and friends.

This event is a combination of Christmas festivities and those of Boxing Day. Decorate the table with pine boughs, holly, mistletoe, juniper berries, cinnamon sticks, oranges with fragrant cloves, bowls of fruit, and tiny Christmas trees. Wrap small boxes with metallic and holiday paper and use for decoration or add small gifts that your guests can open after dinner. You can also fill English "crackers" (colored paper tubes) with candy and small presents. For a unique Boxing Day invitation, write the party information on a piece of paper, fold it up, then place it in a small, wrapped box to hand-deliver to guests.

# classic english toffee

**1 cup (2 sticks) unsalted butter**
**1 cup sugar**
**2 tablespoons water**
**¼ teaspoon salt**
**1 teaspoon vanilla**
**1 bar (3 ounces) premium semisweet chocolate, broken into small pieces**
**1 bar (3 ounces) premium bittersweet chocolate, broken into small pieces**
**½ cup chopped toasted pecans**

1. Line 9-inch square pan with heavy-duty foil, leaving 1-inch overhang on sides.

2. Combine butter, sugar, water, and salt in heavy 2- or 2½-quart saucepan. Bring to a boil over medium heat, stirring frequently. Attach candy thermometer to side of pan. Continue boiling about 20 minutes or until sugar mixture reaches hard-crack stage (305° to 310°F) on candy thermometer, stirring frequently. (Watch closely after temperature reaches 290°F, because temperature will rise quickly and mixture will burn above 310°F.) Remove from heat; stir in vanilla. Immediately pour into prepared pan, spreading to edges. Cool completely.

3. Microwave chocolates in small microwavable bowl on MEDIUM (50% power) 5 to 6 minutes or until melted, stirring every 2 minutes.

4. Remove toffee from pan to flat surface. Lay foil flat; spread chocolate evenly over toffee. Sprinkle chocolate with pecans, pressing lightly with fingertips so pecans adhere to chocolate. Refrigerate about 35 minutes or until chocolate is set. Bring to room temperature before breaking toffee.

5. Carefully break toffee into pieces without dislodging pecans. Store in airtight container at room temperature between sheets of waxed paper.

*Makes about 1¼ pounds toffee*

# prime rib with yorkshire pudding and horseradish cream sauce

**3 cloves garlic, minced**
**1 teaspoon black pepper**
**1 (3-rib) beef rib roast, trimmed\* (about 6 to 7 pounds)**
   **Yorkshire Pudding (page 117)**
   **Horseradish Cream Sauce (page 117)**

*\*Ask meat retailer to remove the chine bone for easier carving. Fat should be trimmed to ¼-inch thickness.*

1. Preheat oven to 450°F. Combine garlic and pepper; rub over surfaces of roast.

2. Place roast, bone side down (bones take the place of a meat rack), in shallow roasting pan. Roast 15 minutes. *Reduce oven temperature to 325°F.* Roast 20 minutes per pound for medium or until internal temperature reaches 145°F when tested with meat thermometer inserted into thickest part of roast, not touching bone.

3. Meanwhile, prepare Yorkshire Pudding batter and Horseradish Cream Sauce.

4. When roast has reached desired temperature, transfer to cutting board; cover with foil. *Increase oven temperature to 450°F.* Reserve ¼ cup drippings from roasting pan for Yorkshire Pudding. Let roast stand 10 to 15 minutes before carving. Internal temperature will continue to rise 5° to 10°F during stand time.

5. While pudding is baking, carve roast. Serve roast with Yorkshire Pudding and Horseradish Cream Sauce. *Makes 6 to 8 servings*

# yorkshire pudding

**1 cup milk**
**2 eggs**
**½ teaspoon salt**
**1 cup all-purpose flour**
**¼ cup reserved drippings from roast or unsalted butter**

1. Process milk, eggs, and salt in blender or food processor 15 seconds. Add flour; process 2 minutes. Let batter stand in blender at room temperature 30 minutes to 1 hour.

2. Place reserved meat drippings in 9-inch square baking pan. Place in 450°F oven 5 minutes.

3. Process batter another 10 seconds; pour into hot drippings. Do not stir.

4. Immediately return pan to oven. Bake 20 minutes. *Reduce oven temperature to 350°F;* bake 10 minutes or until pudding is golden brown and puffed. Cut into squares.                                     *Makes 6 to 8 servings*

# horseradish cream sauce

**1 cup cold whipping cream**
**⅓ cup prepared horseradish, undrained**
**2 teaspoons balsamic or red wine vinegar**
**1 teaspoon dry mustard**
**¼ teaspoon sugar**
**⅛ teaspoon salt**

Beat cream until soft peaks form. *Do not overbeat.* Combine horseradish, vinegar, mustard, sugar, and salt in medium bowl. Fold whipped cream into horseradish mixture. Cover and refrigerate about 1 hour. Sauce may be made up to 8 hours before serving.                                     *Makes about 2 cups*

# le reveillon

What was once a simple meal after midnight mass has blossomed into Le Reveillon, a nighttime dinner for French families with many of the same dishes as those served on Christmas Day. Some families use the event to decorate the tree or give presents. Like many other nationalities, the French often decorate with a nativity scene, greenery, and candles.

## gannat (french cheese bread)

**3 tablespoons water**
**1 teaspoon salt**
**2 eggs**
**¼ cup (½ stick) butter, cut up and softened**
**2½ cups all-purpose flour**
**1 teaspoon sugar**
**1 cup (4 ounces) shredded Cheddar or Swiss cheese**
**2 teaspoons active dry yeast**

### Bread Machine Directions

1. Measuring carefully, place all ingredients in bread machine pan in order specified by owner's manual.

2. Program basic or white cycle and desired crust setting; press start. (Do not use delay cycle.) Remove baked bread from pan; cool on wire rack.

*Makes 1 (1½-pound) loaf (12 to 16 servings)*

# veal oscar with tarragon bearnaise

**Tarragon Bearnaise (page 120)**
16 **fresh asparagus spears, ends trimmed**
 1 **pound lean veal cutlets or veal scaloppine**
¼ **teaspoon salt**
¼ **teaspoon black pepper**
¼ **cup plus 2 tablespoons all-purpose flour**
 3 **tablespoons butter or margarine, divided**
 2 **tablespoons vegetable oil, divided**
 3 **tablespoons white wine**
½ **pound fresh lump crabmeat**
 2 **tablespoons chopped fresh parsley**
 1 **lemon, cut into wedges**

1. Prepare Tarragon Bearnaise; pour into 1-cup glass measuring cup. To keep sauce warm in bain-marie or water bath, bring 2 inches water to a boil in 2-quart baking dish or deep skillet over high heat. Reduce heat to low; place measuring cup with sauce in water. Keep sauce in hot water until ready to serve.

2. To steam asparagus, rinse spears and place in basket. Place basket in large saucepan; add 1 inch water. (Water should not touch bottom of basket.) Cover. Bring to a boil over high heat; steam asparagus 6 to 8 minutes until crisp-tender. Plunge asparagus into ice water to stop cooking; drain and set aside.

3. Pound veal with meat mallet to ¼-inch thickness. Cut veal into serving-size pieces; sprinkle with salt and pepper. Place flour in shallow bowl; dredge veal, 1 piece at a time, in flour.

4. Place 1 tablespoon each butter and oil in large skillet; heat over medium-high heat until butter melts. Add ½ of veal pieces; brown 2 minutes per side or until lightly browned, turning once. Transfer veal to warm serving platter; tent with foil to keep warm. Repeat with 1 tablespoon butter, remaining oil, and veal.

5. To deglaze skillet, pour wine into skillet. Cook over medium-high heat 2 minutes, stirring to scrape up browned bits; pour over browned veal. Set aside.

6. Pick out any shell or cartilage from crabmeat; discard. Flake crab with fork.

7. Melt remaining 1 tablespoon butter in same skillet over medium-high heat. Add crab and parsley; squeeze juice from lemon over crab. Cook and stir until hot.

8. To serve, arrange veal, crab mixture, and asparagus on 4 warm serving plates; top with Tarragon Bearnaise.                    *Makes 4 servings*

*continued on page 120*

*veal oscar with tarragon bearnaise,* continued

## tarragon bearnaise

**3 tablespoons finely chopped shallots**
**2 tablespoons** *each* **white wine and white wine vinegar**
**1 tablespoon chopped fresh tarragon**
 **Dash red pepper flakes**
**2 egg yolks**
 **Dash salt**
**½ cup (1 stick) butter, cut into ½-inch cubes, divided**

1. Combine first 5 ingredients in small saucepan; bring to a boil over high heat. Cook 3 minutes. Strain mixture through fine-meshed sieve; discard solids.

2. Beat egg yolks and salt in top of double boiler with wire whisk; gradually add tarragon mixture, stirring constantly. Add about ⅓ of butter to egg mixture.

3. Fill bottom pan of double boiler with water to 1 inch below level of top pan. Bring water just to a boil; reduce heat to low. Place top of double boiler over hot water; cook until butter melts, stirring constantly with wire whisk.

4. Add another ⅓ of butter, stirring constantly. As sauce thickens, whisk in remaining butter. Cook until instant-read thermometer inserted into sauce, but not touching bottom of pan, registers 160°F.                     *Makes ¾ cup*

# french carrot medley

**2 cups fresh or frozen sliced carrots**
**¾ cup unsweetened orange juice**
**1 can (4 ounces) sliced mushrooms, undrained**
**4 ribs celery, sliced**
**2 tablespoons chopped onion**
**½ teaspoon dill weed**
**2 teaspoons cornstarch**
**¼ cup cold water**

Combine all ingredients except cornstarch and water in medium saucepan. Simmer, covered, 12 to 15 minutes or until carrots are tender. Combine cornstarch with water in small bowl. Stir into vegetable mixture; cook and stir until mixture thickens and bubbles.                     *Makes 6 servings*

# an old-world christmas

Celebrating the season is a month-long tradition in Germany, with festivities culminating on Christmas Eve, the night the Christmas tree is unveiled. Children are not allowed to see the tree until a bell is rung and it is brought out, fully decorated with cars, trains, angels, tinsel, lights, and ornaments. Families sing Christmas carols and place presents underneath. The night later gives way to a feast so lavish that the evening is often called "Dickbauch," or "fat stomach." Legend has it that those who do not eat well will be haunted by demons during the night.

Invite guests to an old-world party by printing out an invitation, leaving the front blank. Then glue greenery to the front in the shape of a wreath. Clippings from your tree, mistletoe, and ivy are easy choices to work with.

On the day of the party, decorate with nuts, fruits, greenery, marzipan, and adorable carved, wooden figurines of angels, trees, and Santa. Don't forget candles and trimmings.

# holiday stollen

1½ cups (3 sticks) unsalted butter, softened
4 egg yolks
½ cup granulated sugar
1 teaspoon salt
   Grated peel of 1 lemon
   Grated peel of 1 orange
1 teaspoon vanilla
2½ cups hot milk (120° to 130°F)
8 to 8½ cups all-purpose flour
2 packages active dry yeast
½ cup golden raisins
½ cup candied orange peel
½ cup candied lemon peel
½ cup chopped red candied cherries
½ cup chopped green candied cherries
½ cup chopped almonds
1 egg, beaten
   Powdered sugar

1. Beat butter, egg yolks, granulated sugar, salt, lemon peel, orange peel, and vanilla in large bowl until light and fluffy. Slowly add milk; mix thoroughly. Add 2 cups flour and yeast; mix well. When mixture is smooth, add enough remaining flour, ½ cup at a time, until dough forms and can be lifted out of bowl. Lightly flour work surface; knead dough until smooth and elastic, about 10 minutes. Mix raisins, candied orange and lemon peels, cherries, and almonds in medium bowl; knead fruit mixture into dough.

2. Place dough in greased bowl, cover with plastic wrap and let rise in warm place about 1 hour or until doubled in bulk.

3. Grease 2 large baking sheets. Turn dough out onto floured work surface. Divide dough in half. Place one half back in bowl; cover and set aside. Cut remaining half into thirds. Roll each third into 12-inch rope. Place on prepared baking sheet. Braid ropes together. Repeat procedure with remaining dough.

4. Brush beaten egg on braids. Let braids stand at room temperature about 1 hour or until doubled in bulk.

5. Preheat oven to 350°F. Bake braids about 45 minutes or until golden brown and sound hollow when tapped. Remove to wire rack to cool. Sprinkle with powdered sugar before serving. *Makes 2 braided loaves*

# german apple pancake

     ¼ **cup (½ stick) butter**
 1 ½ **teaspoons ground cinnamon, divided**
     2 **large cooking apples,* peeled and thinly sliced (about 3 cups)**
     3 **eggs, beaten**
     ½ **cup thawed frozen unsweetened apple juice concentrate**
     ½ **cup all-purpose flour**
     ¼ **cup half-and-half or heavy cream**
     1 **teaspoon vanilla**
     ¼ **teaspoon ground nutmeg**
     ⅛ **teaspoon salt**
         **Apple Cream (recipe follows)**

*Use Jonathan, Rome Beauty, or McIntosh.

Preheat oven to 450°F. Melt butter with ½ teaspoon cinnamon in 9- or 10-inch ovenproof skillet.** Add apples; cook and stir until tender, about 4 minutes. Place eggs, apple juice concentrate, flour, half-and-half, vanilla, remaining 1 teaspoon cinnamon, nutmeg, and salt in food processor container; cover and process until smooth. Pour over apples. Bake 10 minutes or until pancake is set in center. Meanwhile, prepare Apple Cream. Cut pancake into wedges. Serve warm or at room temperature with cream.                    *Makes 6 servings*

**If ovenproof skillet is unavailable, use regular skillet. Cook apple mixture as directed; spoon into 9-inch pie plate. Continue as directed.

# apple cream

     ½ **cup plain yogurt**
     2 **tablespoons thawed frozen unsweetened apple juice**
         **concentrate**
     ½ **teaspoon vanilla**

Combine all ingredients; mix until well blended.

# holiday recipes

**What would Christmas be** without special foods? Pies and cakes and cookies, appetizers, punches and spiced beverages—it's a feast for the senses. The delectable smells that waft throughout the house signify the comforts of home at the holidays.

Here you'll find many yummy yuletide recipes to tempt the palate and warm the tummy. If Grandma doesn't already know how to make these wonderful dishes, she'll surely want the recipes!

# party starters

## cranberry-orange snack mix

**2 cups oatmeal cereal squares**
**2 cups corn cereal squares**
**2 cups mini pretzels**
**1 cup whole almonds**
**¼ cup (½ stick) butter**
**⅓ cup frozen orange juice concentrate, thawed**
**3 tablespoons packed brown sugar**
**1 teaspoon ground cinnamon**
**¾ teaspoon ground ginger**
**¼ teaspoon ground nutmeg**
**⅔ cup dried cranberries or raisins**

1. Preheat oven to 250°F. Spray 13×9-inch baking pan with nonstick cooking spray.

2. Combine cereal squares, pretzels and almonds in large bowl; set aside.

3. Melt butter in medium microwavable bowl at HIGH 45 to 60 seconds. Stir in orange juice concentrate, brown sugar, cinnamon, ginger and nutmeg until blended. Pour over cereal mixture; stir well to coat. Place in prepared pan and spread in single layer.

4. Bake 50 minutes, stirring every 10 minutes. Stir in cranberries. Let cool in pan on wire rack, leaving uncovered until mixture is crisp. Store in airtight container or resealable plastic food storage bags.          *Makes 8 cups snack mix*

*cranberry-orange snack mix*

# cheese pinecones

**2 cups (8 ounces) shredded Swiss cheese**
**½ cup (1 stick) butter or margarine, softened**
**3 tablespoons milk**
**2 tablespoons dry sherry or milk**
**⅛ teaspoon ground red pepper**
**1 cup finely chopped blanched almonds**
**¾ cup sliced almonds**
**½ cup whole almonds**
**Fresh rosemary sprig for garnish (optional)**
**Assorted crackers**

1. Beat cheese, butter, milk, sherry and red pepper in medium bowl until smooth; stir in chopped almonds.

2. Divide mixture into 2 equal portions; shape each into tapered oval to resemble pinecone. Insert sliced and whole almonds into cones. Cover; refrigerate 2 to 3 hours or until firm.

3. Arrange Cheese Pinecones on wooden board or serving plate. Garnish with rosemary, if desired. Serve with assorted crackers.

*Makes 12 to 16 appetizer servings*

*cheese pinecones*

# festive nachos

**5 ounces of tortilla chips**
**3 cups Mexican blend shredded cheese**
**2 cups French's® French Fried Onions**
**1 cup chopped plum tomatoes**
**½ cup sliced black olives**

1. Layer chips, cheese, French Fried Onions, tomatoes and olives on microwave-safe plate. Microwave on HIGH 2 to 3 minutes or until cheese melts.

2. Serve with prepared salsa and guacamole if desired.      *Makes 4 servings*

**Prep Time:** 5 minutes
**Cook Time:** 2 to 3 minutes

# hot pepper cranberry jelly appetizer

**½ cup canned whole cranberry sauce**
**¼ cup apricot fruit spread**
**1 teaspoon sugar**
**1 teaspoon cider vinegar**
**½ teaspoon dried red pepper flakes**
**½ teaspoon grated fresh ginger**
   **Crackers and cheeses**

1. Combine cranberry sauce, fruit spread, sugar, vinegar and red pepper flakes in small saucepan. Cook over medium heat until sugar has dissolved; do not boil. Transfer to bowl to cool completely. Stir in ginger.

2. To serve, top crackers with cheese and dollop of cranberry-apricot mixture.
*Makes 16 appetizer servings*

# little christmas pizzas

⅓ cup olive oil
1 tablespoon **TABASCO®** brand Pepper Sauce
2 large cloves garlic, minced
1 teaspoon dried rosemary, crushed
1 (16-ounce) package hot roll mix with yeast packet*
1¼ cups hot water**
Flour

**Toppings**
1 large tomato, diced
¼ cup crumbled goat cheese
2 tablespoons chopped fresh parsley
½ cup shredded mozzarella cheese
½ cup pitted green olives
⅓ cup roasted red pepper strips
½ cup chopped artichoke hearts
½ cup cherry tomatoes, sliced into wedges
⅓ cup sliced green onions

*Check hot roll mix package directions for dough rising time.*

**Check hot roll mix package directions for temperature of water.*

Combine olive oil, TABASCO® Sauce, garlic and rosemary in small bowl. Combine hot roll mix, yeast packet, hot water and 2 tablespoons TABASCO® Sauce mixture in large bowl; stir until dough pulls away from side of bowl. Turn dough onto lightly floured surface; shape dough into ball. Knead until smooth, adding additional flour as necessary.

Preheat oven to 425°F. Cut dough into quarters; cut each quarter into 10 equal pieces. Roll each piece into ball. On large cookie sheet, press each ball into 2-inch round. Brush each with remaining TABASCO® Sauce mixture. Arrange as desired approximately 2 teaspoons toppings on each dough round. Bake 12 minutes or until dough is lightly browned and puffed.          *Makes 40 appetizer servings*

# guacamole ring

**2 envelopes unflavored gelatin**
**1 cup cold water**
**2 ripe medium avocados, mashed**
**1 cup prepared HIDDEN VALLEY® The Original Ranch® Dressing**
**3 tablespoons lemon juice**
**1 tablespoon finely chopped onion**
**Dash hot pepper sauce**

In small saucepan, soften gelatin in $\frac{1}{2}$ cup of the water; stir over low heat until dissolved. Stir in remaining $\frac{1}{2}$ cup water. In large bowl, combine avocados, salad dressing, lemon juice, onion and pepper sauce; stir in gelatin mixture. Pour into $3\frac{1}{2}$- or 4-cup mold; refrigerate until firm. Just before serving, unmold onto serving platter. Serve with crackers or raw vegetables. Or pour mixture into $9\times3$-inch loaf pan and refrigerate until firm. Unmold, slice and serve as first course appetizer.

*Makes 8 to 10 servings*

# holiday appetizer puffs

**1 sheet frozen puff pastry, thawed ($\frac{1}{2}$ of 17$\frac{1}{4}$-ounce package)**
**2 tablespoons olive or vegetable oil**
**Toppings: grated Parmesan cheese, sesame seeds, poppy seeds, dried dill weed, dried basil leaves, paprika, drained capers, pimiento-stuffed green olive slices**

1. Preheat oven to 425°F. Roll pastry on lightly floured surface to 13-inch square. Cut into shapes with cookie cutters (simple-shaped cutters work best). Place on ungreased baking sheets.

2. Brush cut-outs lightly with oil. Decorate with desired toppings.

3. Bake 6 to 8 minutes or until golden. Serve warm or at room temperature.

*Makes about 1$\frac{1}{2}$ dozen appetizers*

*holiday appetizer puffs*

# pesto cheese wreath

**Parsley-Basil Pesto\* (recipe follows)**
**3 packages (8 ounces each) cream cheese, softened**
**½ cup mayonnaise**
**¼ cup whipping cream or half-and-half**
**1 teaspoon sugar**
**1 teaspoon onion salt**
**⅓ cup chopped roasted red peppers\*\* or pimiento, drained**
**Pimiento strips and Italian flat-leaf parsley leaves (optional)**
**Assorted crackers and cut-up vegetables**

*\*One-half cup purchased pesto can be substituted for Parsley-Basil Pesto.*

*\*\*Look for roasted red peppers packed in cans or jars in the Italian food section of the supermarket.*

1. Prepare Parsley-Basil Pesto; set aside. Beat cream cheese and mayonnaise in medium bowl until smooth; beat in whipping cream, sugar and onion salt.

2. Line 5-cup ring mold with plastic wrap. Spoon half of cheese mixture into prepared mold; spread evenly. Spread Parsley-Basil Pesto evenly over cheese mixture; top with chopped red peppers. Spoon remaining cheese mixture over peppers; spread evenly. Cover; refrigerate until cheese mixture is firm, 8 hours or overnight.

3. Uncover mold; invert onto serving plate. Carefully remove plastic wrap. Smooth top and sides of wreath with spatula. Garnish with pimiento strips and parsley leaves, if desired. Serve with assorted crackers and vegetables.

*Makes 16 to 24 appetizer servings*

# parsley-basil pesto

**2 cups fresh parsley leaves**
**¼ cup pine nuts or slivered almonds**
**2 tablespoons grated Parmesan cheese**
**2 cloves garlic, peeled**
**1 tablespoon dried basil leaves, crushed**
**¼ teaspoon salt**
**2 tablespoons olive or vegetable oil**

Process all ingredients except oil in food processor or blender until finely chopped. With machine running, add oil gradually, processing until mixture is smooth.

*Makes about ½ cup*

*pesto cheese wreath*

# date-nut cream cheese spread

**½ cup hazelnuts**
**1 package (8 ounces) Neufchâtel cheese, softened**
**½ cup vanilla-flavored low-fat yogurt**
**1 tablespoon packed brown sugar**
**1 teaspoon vanilla**
**¼ teaspoon ground cinnamon**
**½ cup chopped pitted dates**

1. Preheat oven to 350°F.

2. To toast hazelnuts, spread in single layer on baking sheet. Bake 10 to 12 minutes or until toasted and skins begin to flake off; let cool slightly. Wrap hazelnuts in heavy kitchen towel; rub towel back and forth to remove as much of skins as possible.

3. Place hazelnuts in food processor; process until coarsely chopped.

4. Beat cheese in medium bowl with electric mixer at medium speed until smooth. Beat in yogurt, brown sugar, vanilla and cinnamon. Stir in dates. Stir in nuts just before serving. *Makes 1½ cups*

**NOTE:** Spread can be covered and refrigerated up to 1 week. Spread will remain soft when refrigerated.

# nicole's cheddar crisps

**1¾ cups all-purpose flour**
**½ cup yellow cornmeal**
**¾ teaspoon sugar**
**¾ teaspoon salt**
**½ teaspoon baking soda**
**½ cup (1 stick) butter or margarine**
**1½ cups (6 ounces) shredded sharp Cheddar cheese**
**½ cup cold water**
**2 tablespoons white vinegar**
**Coarsely ground black pepper**

1. Mix flour, cornmeal, sugar, salt and baking soda in large bowl. Cut in butter with pastry blender or two knives until mixture resembles coarse crumbs. Stir in cheese, water and vinegar with fork until mixture forms soft dough. Cover dough; refrigerate 1 hour or freeze 30 minutes until firm.*

2. Preheat oven to 375°F. Grease 2 large cookie sheets. Divide dough into 4 pieces. Roll each piece into paper-thin circle (about 13 inches in diameter) on floured surface. Sprinkle with pepper; press pepper firmly into dough.

3. Cut each circle into 8 wedges; place on prepared cookie sheets. Bake about 10 minutes or until crisp. Store in airtight container for up to 3 days.

*Makes 32 crisps*

*Dough may be frozen at this point. To prepare, thaw in refrigerator and proceed as directed.*

# bacon cheese spread

**½ cup FLEISCHMANN'S® Original Margarine, softened**
**¼ cup grated Parmesan cheese**
**¼ cup real bacon bits**
**¼ cup minced onion**

1. Blend margarine, cheese, bacon and onion in small bowl with mixer at medium speed. Cover and store in refrigerator.

2. Serve as a topping for baked potatoes or as a spread for toasted Italian bread.

*Makes about 1 cup*

**Preparation Time:** 10 minutes
**Total Time:** 10 minutes

# cranberry-barbecue chicken wings

**3 pounds chicken wings**
**Salt and black pepper**
**1 container (12 ounces) cranberry-orange relish**
**½ cup barbecue sauce**
**2 tablespoons quick-cooking tapioca**
**1 tablespoon prepared mustard**

## Slow Cooker Directions

1. Preheat broiler. Rinse chicken and pat dry. Cut off and discard wing tips. Cut each wing in half at joint. Place chicken on rack in broiler pan; season with salt and pepper. Broil 4 to 5 inches from heat 10 to 12 minutes or until browned, turning once. Transfer chicken to slow cooker.

2. Stir together relish, barbecue sauce, tapioca and mustard in small bowl. Pour over chicken. Cover; cook on LOW 4 to 5 hours.

*Makes about 16 appetizer servings*

**Prep Time:** 20 minutes
**Cook Time:** 4 to 5 hours

*bacon cheese spread*

# roasted sweet pepper tapas

**2 red bell peppers (8 ounces each)**
**2 tablespoons olive oil**
**1 clove garlic, minced**
**1 teaspoon chopped fresh oregano or ½ teaspoon dried**
    **oregano leaves, crushed**
    **Garlic bread (optional)**
    **Fresh oregano sprig for garnish (optional)**

1. Cover broiler pan with foil. Adjust rack so that broiler pan is about 4 inches from heat source. Preheat broiler. Place peppers on foil. Broil 15 to 20 minutes or until blackened on all sides, turning peppers every 5 minutes with tongs.

2. To steam peppers and loosen skin, place blackened peppers in paper bag. Close bag; set aside to cool about 15 to 20 minutes.

3. To peel peppers, cut around core, twist and remove. Cut peppers in half; place pepper halves on cutting board. Peel off skin with paring knife; rinse under cold water to remove seeds.

4. Lay halves flat and slice lengthwise into ¼-inch strips.

5. Transfer pepper strips to glass jar. Add oil, garlic and oregano. Close lid; shake to blend. Marinate at least 1 hour. Serve on plates with garlic bread, if desired, or refrigerate in jar up to 1 week. Garnish, if desired.

*Makes 6 appetizer servings*

**TIP:** Use this roasting technique for all types of sweet and hot peppers. Broiling time will vary depending on size of pepper. When handling hot peppers, such as Anaheim, jalapeño, poblano or serrano, wear plastic disposable gloves and use caution to prevent irritation of skin or eyes. Green bell peppers do not work as well since their skins are thinner.

*roasted sweet pepper tapas*

# gingerbread caramel corn

**10 cups popped, lightly salted popcorn (about ⅔ cup unpopped *or*
1 package [3½ ounces] microwave popcorn)
1 cup lightly salted roasted cashews
1 cup packed dark brown sugar
½ cup (1 stick) butter
¼ cup light corn syrup
1 teaspoon ground ginger
1 teaspoon ground cinnamon
½ teaspoon baking soda**

1. Preheat oven to 250°F. Line 17×11-inch shallow roasting pan with foil or use disposable foil roasting pan.

2. Combine popcorn and cashews in prepared pan; set aside.

3. Combine brown sugar, butter and syrup in heavy 1½- or 2-quart saucepan. Bring to a boil over medium heat, stirring constantly. Wash down sugar crystals with pastry brush, if necessary.

4. Attach candy thermometer to side of pan, making sure bulb is submerged in sugar mixture but not touching bottom of pan. Continue boiling, without stirring, about 5 minutes or until sugar mixture reaches soft-crack stage (290°F) on candy thermometer. Remove from heat; stir in ginger, cinnamon and baking soda. Immediately drizzle sugar mixture slowly over popcorn mixture; stir until evenly coated.

5. Bake 1 hour, stirring quickly every 15 minutes. Transfer to large baking sheet lined with foil; spread caramel corn in single layer. Cool completely, about 10 minutes. Store in airtight container at room temperature.

*Makes about 10 cups caramel corn*

*gingerbread caramel corn*

# eggplant appetizer

**1 medium eggplant (about 1 pound)**
**¼ pound lean ground beef**
**¼ cup finely chopped onion**
**1 large clove garlic, minced**
**1 large tomato, chopped**
**1 small green bell pepper, finely chopped**
**¼ cup diced green olives**
**2 tablespoons olive oil**
**1 teaspoon white wine vinegar**
**1 tablespoon chopped fresh oregano *or* 1 teaspoon dried**
    **oregano leaves**
**Salt and black pepper**

1. Preheat oven to 350°F. Pierce eggplant with fork; place in shallow baking pan. Bake 1 hour or until skin is wrinkled and eggplant is soft. Set aside until cool enough to handle.

2. Meanwhile, brown ground beef in medium skillet. Drain. Add onion and garlic; cook until tender.

3. Peel eggplant; cut into small cubes. Combine eggplant, ground beef mixture, tomato, bell pepper and olives in medium bowl. Whisk together oil, vinegar and oregano in small bowl. Add to eggplant mixture; mix lightly. Season with salt and black pepper to taste.

4. Serve with toasted pita wedges. *Makes about 8 servings*

# lemon dill seafood spread

**2 packages (8 ounces each) light cream cheese, at room temperature**
**½ cup bottled lemon butter dill cooking sauce**
**½ cup thinly sliced green onions**
**½ teaspoon lemon pepper seasoning**
**16 ounces surimi seafood, crab- or lobster-flavored, flake- or coarsely chopped chunk-style, drained**

Blend cream cheese, cooking sauce, green onions and lemon pepper seasoning in electric mixer or by hand. Stir in surimi seafood; press mixture into a 4-cup mold lined with plastic wrap. Cover and refrigerate several hours or overnight. Unmold on serving platter and garnish, if desired, with fresh dill or other fresh herbs. Serve with crackers or melba toast. *Makes 4 cups*

*Favorite recipe from* **National Fisheries Institute**

# brats in beer

**1½ pounds bratwurst (about 5 or 6 links)**
**1 can or bottle (12 ounces) beer (not dark)**
**1 medium onion, thinly sliced**
**2 tablespoons packed brown sugar**
**2 tablespoons red wine or cider vinegar**
**Spicy brown mustard**
**Cocktail rye bread**

**Slow Cooker Directions**

1. Combine bratwurst, beer, onion, brown sugar and vinegar in slow cooker.

2. Cover; cook on LOW 4 to 5 hours.

3. Remove bratwurst from cooking liquid. Cut into ½-inch-thick slices. For mini open-faced sandwiches, spread mustard on cocktail rye bread. Top with bratwurst and onion slices from slow cooker. *Makes 30 to 36 appetizers*

**Tip:** Choose a light-tasting beer for cooking brats. Hearty ales might leave the meat tasting slightly bitter.

**Prep Time:** 5 minutes
**Cook Time:** 4 to 5 hours

# festive taco cups

**1 tablespoon vegetable oil**
**½ cup chopped onion**
**½ pound ground turkey or ground beef**
**1 clove garlic, minced**
**½ teaspoon dried oregano leaves**
**½ teaspoon chili powder or taco seasoning**
**¼ teaspoon salt**
**1¼ cups shredded taco-flavored cheese or Mexican cheese blend, divided**
**1 can (11½ ounces) refrigerated corn breadstick dough**
**Chopped fresh tomato and sliced green onion for garnish (optional)**

1. Heat oil in large skillet over medium heat. Add onion and cook until tender. Add turkey; cook until turkey is no longer pink, stirring occasionally. Stir in garlic, oregano, chili powder and salt. Remove from heat and stir in ½ cup cheese; set aside.

2. Preheat oven to 375°F. Lightly grease 24 miniature (1¾-inch) muffin pan cups. Remove dough from container but do not unroll. Separate dough into 8 pieces at perforations. Divide each piece into 3 pieces; roll or pat each piece into 3-inch circle. Press circles into prepared muffin pan cups.

3. Fill each cup with 1½ to 2 teaspoons turkey mixture. Bake 10 minutes. Sprinkle tops of taco cups with remaining ¾ cup cheese; bake 2 to 3 minutes more until cheese is melted. Garnish with tomato and green onion, if desired.

*Makes 24 taco cups*

*festive taco cups*

# stuffed mushrooms with tomato sauce

**Tomato Sauce (recipe follows)**
**1 pound extra-lean (90% lean) ground beef**
**¼ cup *each* finely chopped onion and green bell pepper**
**1 large clove garlic, minced**
**2 tablespoons finely chopped fresh parsley**
**2 teaspoons finely chopped fresh basil**
**1 teaspoon finely chopped fresh oregano**
**½ teaspoon salt**
**Dash black pepper**
**12 very large mushrooms**
**¼ cup (1 ounce) grated Parmesan cheese**
**4½ cups cooked spaghetti (optional)**
**Fresh basil leaves for garnish (optional)**

1. Prepare Tomato Sauce; set aside. Preheat oven to 350°F.

2. Combine ground beef, onion, bell pepper, garlic, parsley, basil, oregano, salt and black pepper in medium bowl; mix lightly. Remove stems from mushrooms; finely chop stems. Add to ground beef mixture. Stuff into mushroom caps, rounding tops.

3. Pour Tomato Sauce into shallow casserole dish large enough to hold mushrooms in single layer. Place mushrooms, stuffing side up, in sauce; cover.

4. Bake 20 minutes; remove cover. Sprinkle with Parmesan cheese. Continue baking, uncovered, 15 minutes. Serve with spaghetti and garnish with additional fresh basil leaves, if desired.                                          *Makes 6 servings*

# tomato sauce

**2 cans (14½ ounces) tomatoes, chopped, undrained**
**Dash hot pepper sauce**
**1 teaspoon finely chopped fresh marjoram *or* ½ teaspoon dried marjoram leaves, crushed**
**1 teaspoon fennel seeds, crushed**
**Salt and black pepper**

Combine all ingredients except salt and black pepper in medium saucepan. Bring to a boil. Reduce heat; simmer 5 minutes. Season with salt and black pepper to taste.

*stuffed mushrooms with tomato sauce*

# cranberry-glazed brie

**Cornmeal**
¾ **cup canned whole berry cranberry sauce, well drained**
¼ **teaspoon dry mustard**
⅛ **teaspoon ground ginger**
⅛ **teaspoon ground cloves**
⅛ **teaspoon ground allspice**
1 **package (17¼ ounces) frozen puff pastry sheets, thawed**
1 **round (15 ounces) fully ripened Brie cheese**
1 **egg**
1 **tablespoon water**
  **Green, red and yellow food colorings**
  **Sliced pears and/or assorted crackers**

1. Preheat oven to 400°F. Lightly sprinkle baking sheet with cornmeal.

2. Combine cranberry sauce, mustard and spices; mix well.

3. Place 1 puff pastry sheet on lightly floured surface; roll out pastry with rolling pin to about 2 inches larger than diameter of cheese round. Place cheese in center of pastry. With sharp knife, cut away excess pastry, leaving 1-inch rim around bottom of cheese; reserve trimmings. Place pastry and cheese on prepared baking sheet. Spread cranberry mixture onto top of cheese to within 1 inch of edge.

4. Roll out remaining pastry sheet to completely cover cheese. Place pastry over cheese; trim away excess pastry. (Be sure to leave 1-inch rim of pastry at bottom of cheese.) With sharp knife, cut slits in top of pastry to allow steam to vent.

5. Combine egg and water; beat lightly with fork. Brush onto pastry to cover completely. Fold up bottom rim of pastry; press edges together to seal.

6. Cut out leaf shapes or other decorative designs from pastry trimmings. "Glue" cutouts onto top of pastry-covered cheese with remaining egg mixture; brush with food colorings that have been diluted slightly with water.

7. Bake 15 minutes. *Reduce oven temperature to 350°F.* Continue baking 15 to 20 minutes or until pastry is golden brown. Remove to wire rack; let stand 15 minutes before cutting. Serve warm with pear slices and/or crackers.

*Makes 12 appetizer servings*

# lamb meatballs with tomato mint dip

**1½ cups fine bulgur**
**3 cups cold water**
**2 pounds ground American lamb**
**1 cup minced fresh parsley**
**2 medium onions, minced**
**1 tablespoon salt**
**½ teaspoon ground black pepper**
**½ teaspoon ground allspice**
**½ teaspoon ground cinnamon**
**½ teaspoon ground nutmeg**
**¼ to ½ teaspoon ground red pepper (to taste)**
**1 piece fresh ginger, about 2×1-inch, peeled and minced**
**1 cup ice water**
**Tomato Mint Dip (recipe follows)**

In medium bowl, pour cold water over bulgur to cover; let soak about 10 minutes. Drain and place in fine meshed strainer; squeeze out water.

In large bowl, knead lamb with parsley, onions, seasonings and ginger. Add bulgur; knead well. Add ice water to keep mixture smooth. Use about 1 teaspoon meat mixture to make bite-sized meatballs. Place on ungreased jelly-roll pan. Bake in preheated 375°F oven 20 minutes. Meanwhile, prepare Tomato Mint Dip.

Place meatballs in serving bowl; keep warm. Serve hot with dip.

*Makes 10 dozen meatballs*

# tomato mint dip

**2 cans (15 ounces each) tomato sauce with tomato bits**
**1½ teaspoons ground allspice**
**1 teaspoon dried mint**

In small saucepan, heat all ingredients about 5 minutes to blend flavors.

*Favorite recipe from **American Lamb Council***

# spinach-artichoke party cups

**Nonstick cooking spray**
**36 (3-inch) wonton wrappers**
**1 can (8½ ounces) artichoke hearts, drained and chopped**
**½ package (10 ounces) frozen chopped spinach, thawed and squeezed dry**
**1 cup shredded Monterey Jack cheese**
**½ cup grated Parmesan cheese**
**½ cup mayonnaise**
**1 clove garlic, minced**

1. Preheat oven to 300°F. Spray miniature muffin pan lightly with cooking spray. Press 1 wonton wrapper into each cup; spray lightly with cooking spray. Bake about 9 minutes or until light golden brown. Remove shells from muffin pan; set aside to cool. Repeat with remaining wonton wrappers.*

2. Meanwhile, combine artichoke hearts, spinach, cheeses, mayonnaise and garlic in medium bowl; mix well.

3. Fill each wonton cup with about 1½ teaspoons spinach-artichoke mixture. Place filled cups on baking sheet. Bake about 7 minutes or until heated through. Serve immediately.                    *Makes 36 appetizers*

*Wonton cups may be prepared up to one week in advance. Cool completely and store in an airtight container.*

**TIP:** If you have leftover spinach-artichoke mixture after filling the wonton cups, place the mixture in a shallow ovenproof dish and bake it at 350°F until hot and bubbly. Serve it with bread or crackers.

*spinach-artichoke party cups*

# shrimp toast

**12 large shrimp, shelled and deveined, leaving tails intact**
**1 egg**
**2 tablespoons plus 1½ teaspoons cornstarch**
**¼ teaspoon salt**
  **Dash black pepper**
**3 slices white sandwich bread, crusts removed, quartered**
**1 hard-cooked egg yolk, cut into ½-inch pieces**
**1 slice (1 ounce) cooked ham, cut into ½-inch pieces**
**1 green onion with top, finely chopped**
  **Vegetable oil for frying**
  **Hard-cooked egg half and Green Onion Curls (recipe follows)**
    **for garnish (optional)**

1. Cut deep slit down back of each shrimp; press gently with fingers to flatten. Beat 1 egg, cornstarch, salt and pepper in large bowl until blended. Add shrimp; toss to coat well.

2. Place 1 shrimp, cut side down, on each bread piece; press shrimp gently into bread.

3. Brush or rub small amount of leftover egg mixture onto each shrimp.

4. Place one piece each of egg yolk, ham and scant ¼ teaspoon onion on top of each shrimp.

5. Heat oil in wok or large skillet over medium-high heat to 375°F. Add three or four bread pieces at a time; cook 1 to 2 minutes on each side or until golden. Drain on paper towels. Garnish, if desired.

*Makes 12 servings (1 dozen appetizers)*

# green onion curls

**6 to 8 medium green onions with tops**
  **Cold water**
**10 to 12 ice cubes**

1. Trim bulbs (white part) from onions; reserve for another use, if desired. Trim remaining stems (green part) to 4-inch lengths.

2. Using sharp scissors, cut each section of green stems lengthwise into very thin strips down to beginning of stems, cutting 6 to 8 strips from each stem section.

3. Fill large bowl about half full with cold water. Add green onions and ice cubes. Refrigerate until onions curl, about 1 hour; drain. *Makes 6 to 8 curls*

*shrimp toast*

# star-studded entrées

## crown roast of pork with peach stuffing

> 1 (7- to 8-pound) crown roast of pork (12 to 16 ribs)
> 1½ cups water
> 1 cup FLEISCHMANN'S® Original Margarine, divided
> 1 (15-ounce) package seasoned bread cubes
> 1 cup chopped celery
> 2 medium onions, chopped
> 1 (16-ounce) can sliced peaches, drained and chopped, liquid reserved
> ½ cup seedless raisins

1. Place crown roast, bone tips up, on rack in shallow roasting pan. Make a ball of foil and press into cavity to hold open. Wrap bone tips in foil. Roast at 325°F, uncovered, for 2 hours; baste with pan drippings occasionally.

2. Heat water and ¾ cup margarine to a boil in large heavy pot; remove from heat. Add bread cubes, tossing lightly with a fork; set aside.

3. Cook and stir celery and onions in remaining margarine in large skillet over medium-high heat until tender, about 5 minutes.

4. Add celery mixture, peaches with liquid and raisins to bread cube mixture, tossing to mix well.

5. Remove foil from center of roast. Spoon stuffing lightly into cavity. Roast 30 to 45 minutes more or until meat thermometer registers 155°F (internal temperature will rise to 160°F upon standing). Cover stuffing with foil, if necessary, to prevent overbrowning. Bake any remaining stuffing in greased, covered casserole during last 30 minutes of roasting. *Makes 12 to 16 servings*

**Preparation Time:** 45 minutes
**Cook Time:** 2 hours and 30 minutes
**Total Time:** 3 hours and 15 minutes

*crown roast of pork with peach stuffing*

# roasted turkey breast with cherry & apple rice stuffing

**3¾ cups water**
**3 boxes UNCLE BEN'S® Long Grain & Wild Rice Butter & Herb Fast Cook Recipe**
**½ cup (1 stick) butter or margarine, divided**
**½ cup dried red tart cherries**
**1 large apple, peeled and chopped (about 1 cup)**
**½ cup sliced almonds, toasted***
**1 bone-in turkey breast (5 to 6 pounds)**

*To toast almonds, place them on a baking sheet. Bake 10 to 12 minutes in preheated 325°F oven or until golden brown, stirring occasionally.*

1. In large saucepan, combine water, rice, contents of seasoning packets, 3 tablespoons butter and cherries. Bring to a boil. Cover; reduce heat to low and simmer 25 minutes or until all water is absorbed. Stir in apple and almonds; set aside.

2. Preheat oven to 325°F. Place turkey breast, skin side down, on rack in roasting pan. Loosely fill breast cavity with rice stuffing. (Place any remaining stuffing in greased baking dish; cover and refrigerate. Bake alongside turkey for 35 to 40 minutes or until heated through.)

3. Place sheet of heavy-duty foil over stuffing, molding it slightly over sides of turkey. Carefully invert turkey, skin side up, on rack. Melt remaining 5 tablespoons butter; brush some of butter over surface of turkey.

4. Roast turkey, uncovered, 1 hour; baste with melted butter. Continue roasting 1 hour 15 minutes to 1 hour 45 minutes, basting occasionally with melted butter, until meat thermometer inserted into center of thickest part of turkey breast, not touching bone, registers 170°F. Let turkey stand, covered, 15 minutes before carving.                    *Makes 6 to 8 servings*

*roasted turkey breast with cherry & apple rice stuffing*

# beef tenderloin with roasted vegetables

**1 beef tenderloin roast (about 3 pounds), well trimmed**
**½ cup chardonnay or other dry white wine**
**½ cup soy sauce**
**2 cloves garlic, sliced**
**1 tablespoon fresh rosemary**
**1 tablespoon Dijon mustard**
**1 teaspoon dry mustard**
**1 pound small red or white potatoes, cut into 1-inch pieces**
**1 pound Brussels sprouts**
**1 package (12 ounces) baby carrots**
**Cider Pan Gravy (page 162, optional)**
**Fresh rosemary for garnish (optional)**

1. Place tenderloin in large resealable plastic food storage bag. Combine wine, soy sauce, garlic, rosemary, Dijon mustard and dry mustard in small bowl. Pour over tenderloin. Seal bag; turn to coat. Marinate in refrigerator 4 to 12 hours, turning several times.

2. Preheat oven to 425°F. Spray 13×9-inch baking pan with nonstick cooking spray. Place potatoes, Brussels sprouts and carrots in pan. Remove tenderloin from marinade. Pour marinade over vegetables; toss to coat well. Cover vegetables with foil. Bake 30 minutes; stir.

3. Place tenderloin on vegetables. Roast, uncovered, 35 to 45 minutes or until internal temperature of tenderloin reaches 135°F for medium rare to 150°F for medium when tested with meat thermometer inserted into thickest part of tenderloin.

4. Transfer tenderloin to cutting board; cover with foil. Let stand 10 to 15 minutes before carving. (Internal temperature will continue to rise 5° to 10°F during stand time.)

5. Stir vegetables; test for doneness and continue to bake if not tender. Transfer to serving bowl; keep warm. Prepare Cider Pan Gravy, if desired. Slice tenderloin; arrange on serving platter with roasted vegetables, gravy and fresh rosemary, if desired. *Makes 10 servings*

*continued on page 162*

*beef tenderloin with roasted vegetables*

*beef tenderloin with roasted vegetables,* continued

## cider pan gravy

**Reserved drippings from roasting pan**
**3 tablespoons all-purpose flour**
**2 cups chicken broth or turkey stock**
**¼ cup heavy whipping cream**
**½ teaspoon salt, or to taste**
**¼ teaspoon freshly ground black pepper**

Pour drippings into measuring cup; spoon off 3 tablespoons of fat and transfer to medium saucepan. Discard rest of fat. Add flour; cook over medium heat 1 minute, stirring constantly. Gradually stir in chicken broth, then defatted reserved drippings. Cook over medium heat 10 minutes, stirring occasionally. Stir in cream, salt and pepper. Season with more salt, if desired.        *Makes 8 to 10 servings*

# holiday baked ham

**1 bone-in smoked ham (8½ pounds)**
**1 can (20 ounces) DOLE® Pineapple Slices**
**1 cup apricot preserves**
**1 teaspoon dry mustard**
**½ teaspoon ground allspice**
   **Whole cloves**
   **Maraschino cherries**

● Preheat oven to 325°F. Remove rind from ham. Place ham on rack in open roasting pan, fat side up. Insert meat thermometer with bulb in thickest part away from fat or bone. Roast ham in oven about 3 hours.

● Drain pineapple slices; reserve syrup. In small saucepan, combine syrup, preserves, mustard and allspice. Bring to a boil; continue boiling, stirring occasionally, 10 minutes. Remove ham from oven, but keep oven hot. Stud ham with cloves; brush with glaze. Using wooden picks, secure pineapple slices and cherries to ham. Brush again with glaze. Return ham to oven. Roast 30 minutes longer or until thermometer registers 160°F (about 25 minutes per pound total cooking time). Brush with glaze 15 minutes before done. Let ham stand 20 minutes before slicing.        *Makes 8 to 10 servings*

# cranberry smothered chicken

**½ cup all-purpose flour**
**Salt and white pepper to taste**
**3 whole chicken breasts, split and skinned**
**¼ cup vegetable oil**
**3 cloves garlic, minced**
**½ cup chicken broth**
**2 tablespoons butter or margarine**
**3 medium onions, coarsely chopped**
**2 medium green bell peppers, cut into thin strips**
**10 large mushrooms, sliced**
**½ cup raspberry or balsamic vinegar**
**1 can (16 ounces) whole berry cranberry sauce**
**1 cup orange juice**
**1 tablespoon cornstarch**
**1 tablespoon Worcestershire sauce**
**Hot cooked rice and steamed fresh asparagus**

1. Combine flour, salt and white pepper in large resealable plastic food storage bag. Add chicken to bag; shake to coat completely with flour mixture.

2. Heat oil in large skillet over medium-high heat. Add garlic; cook until soft. Add chicken; cook until chicken is browned on both sides. Drain drippings from skillet. Add chicken broth; bring to a boil over high heat. Reduce heat to low. Cover; simmer 30 minutes.

3. Melt butter in another large skillet over medium-high heat. Cook and stir onions, bell peppers and mushrooms in hot butter until vegetables are softened. Stir in vinegar, cranberry sauce and orange juice. Reduce heat to medium. Cook and stir about 5 minutes or until cranberry sauce melts and mixture is heated through.

4. Combine cornstarch and Worcestershire sauce with enough water to make a smooth paste; add to sauce and vegetables in skillet. Stir gently over low heat until thickened. Season with salt and white pepper.

5. Arrange chicken, rice and asparagus on individual serving plates. Pour sauce over chicken. Garnish, if desired. *Makes 6 servings*

# marinated pork roast

**½ cup GRANDMA'S® Molasses**
**½ cup Dijon mustard**
**¼ cup tarragon vinegar**
   **Boneless pork loin roast (3 to 4 pounds)**

1. In large plastic bowl, combine molasses, mustard and tarragon vinegar; mix well. Add pork to molasses mixture, turning to coat all sides. Marinate, covered, 1 to 2 hours at room temperature or overnight in refrigerator, turning several times.

2. Heat oven to 325°F. Remove pork from marinade; reserve marinade. Place pork in shallow roasting pan. Cook for 1 to 2 hours or until meat thermometer inserted into thickest part of roast reaches 160°F, basting with marinade every 30 minutes; discard remaining marinade.* Slice roast and garnish, if desired.

*Makes 6 to 8 servings*

*Do not baste during last 5 minutes of cooking.

# turkey breast with barley-cranberry stuffing

   **2 cups chicken broth**
   **1 cup uncooked quick-cooking barley**
   **½ cup *each* chopped onion and dried cranberries**
   **2 tablespoons slivered almonds, toasted**
   **½ teaspoon *each* rubbed sage and garlic-pepper seasoning**
      **Nonstick cooking spray**
   **1 fresh bone-in turkey breast half (about 2 pounds), skinned**
   **⅓ cup finely chopped fresh parsley**

**Slow Cooker Directions**

1. Combine broth, barley, onion, cranberries, almonds, sage and garlic-pepper seasoning in slow cooker.

2. Spray large nonstick skillet with cooking spray. Heat over medium heat until hot. Brown turkey breast on all sides; add to slow cooker. Cover; cook on LOW 4 to 6 hours.

3. Transfer turkey to cutting board; cover with foil and let stand 10 to 15 minutes before carving. Stir parsley into sauce mixture in slow cooker. Serve sliced turkey with sauce and stuffing.

*Makes 6 servings*

*marinated pork roast and baked apple (page 196)*

# roast turkey with herb stuffing

**4 cups cubed soft herb- or garlic-flavored breadsticks**
**1 turkey (8 to 10 pounds)**
**1 tablespoon margarine**
**1½ cups sliced brown mushrooms**
**1 cup chopped onion**
**⅔ cup chopped celery**
**¼ cup chopped fresh parsley**
**1 to 2 tablespoons chopped fresh tarragon**
**1 tablespoon chopped fresh thyme**
**¼ teaspoon black pepper**
**¼ cup chicken broth**
**Red grapes and fresh sage leaves for garnish (optional)**

1. Preheat oven to 350°F. Place cubed breadsticks on nonstick baking sheet. Bake 20 minutes to dry.

2. Remove giblets from turkey. Rinse turkey and cavities; pat dry with paper towels. Melt margarine in large nonstick skillet. Add mushrooms, onion and celery. Cook and stir 5 minutes or until onion is soft and golden; remove from heat. Add parsley, tarragon, thyme, pepper and bread cubes; stir until blended. Gently mix chicken broth into bread cube mixture. Fill turkey cavities with stuffing.

3. Spray roasting pan with nonstick cooking spray. Place turkey, breast side up, in roasting pan. Bake in 350°F oven 3 hours or until meat thermometer inserted into thigh registers 180°F and juices run clear.

4. Transfer turkey to serving platter. Cover loosely with foil; let stand 20 minutes. Remove and discard skin, if desired. Slice turkey and serve with herb stuffing. Garnish with grapes and fresh sage, if desired. *Makes 10 servings*

*roast turkey with herb stuffing*

# roast beef with red wine gravy

**2 tablespoons oil**
**1 sirloin tip roast (3 to 4 pounds)**
**Salt and black pepper**
**2 tablespoons all-purpose flour**
**1 jar (7 ounces) cocktail onions, drained**
**1 can (14½ ounces) beef broth**
**2 tablespoons HOLLAND HOUSE® Red Cooking Wine**
**Sherried Mushrooms (page 192, optional)**

Heat oven to 350°F. Heat oil in Dutch oven. Season roast to taste with salt and pepper; brown on all sides. Remove from Dutch oven. Drain excess fat, reserving ¼ cup drippings in Dutch oven. Sprinkle flour over reserved drippings. Cook over medium heat until lightly browned, stirring constantly. Add roast and onions to Dutch oven. Roast for 1 hour 45 minutes to 2 hours 15 minutes or until desired doneness. Remove roast to cutting board. Let stand 5 to 10 minutes before slicing. Gradually stir in beef broth and cooking wine into Dutch oven. Bring to a boil; reduce heat. Cook until gravy thickens. Slice roast and serve with gravy. Serve with Sherried Mushrooms, if desired. *Makes 6 servings*

# cranberry-glazed ham

**1 (5- to 6-pound) fully cooked spiral sliced ham half\***
**¾ cup cranberry sauce or bottled cranberry chutney**
**¼ cup Dijon or hot Dijon mustard**
**1 teaspoon ground cinnamon**
**¼ teaspoon ground allspice**

*\*A whole ham will be 10 to 12 pounds and serves 24. Double glaze ingredients if using a whole ham.*

Preheat oven to 300°F. Place ham in large roasting pan lined with heavy-duty aluminum foil. Combine cranberry sauce, mustard, cinnamon and allspice; mix well. Spread half of mixture evenly over top of ham (glaze will melt and spread as it cooks). Bake 1 hour; spread remaining cranberry mixture over top of ham. Continue to bake until internal temperature of ham reaches 140°F, about 1 hour. Transfer ham to carving board; let stand 5 minutes before serving. *Makes 10 to 12 servings*

*roast beef with red wine gravy and sherried mushrooms (page 192)*

# sweet jalapeño mustard turkey thighs

**3 turkey thighs, skin removed**
**¾ cup honey mustard**
**½ cup orange juice**
**1 tablespoon cider vinegar**
**1 teaspoon Worcestershire sauce**
**1 to 2 fresh jalapeño peppers,\* finely chopped**
**1 clove garlic, minced**
**½ teaspoon grated orange peel**

*\*Jalapeño peppers can sting and irritate the skin; wear rubber gloves when handling peppers and do not touch eyes. Wash hands after handling.*

### Slow Cooker Directions

Place turkey thighs in single layer in slow cooker. Combine remaining ingredients in large bowl. Pour mixture over turkey thighs. Cover; cook on LOW 5 to 6 hours.

*Makes 6 servings*

# cranberry-glazed cornish hens with wild rice

**1 box UNCLE BEN'S® Long Grain & Wild Rice Fast Cook Recipe**
**½ cup sliced celery**
**⅓ cup slivered almonds (optional)**
**1 can (8 ounces) jellied cranberry sauce, divided**
**4 Cornish hens, thawed (about 1 pound each)**
**2 tablespoons olive oil, divided**

1. Heat oven to 425°F. Prepare rice according to package directions. Stir in celery, almonds and ½ of cranberry sauce; cool.

2. Spoon about ¾ cup rice mixture into cavity of each hen. Tie drumsticks together with cotton string. Place hens on rack in roasting pan. Brush each hen with some of the oil. Roast 35 to 45 minutes or until juices run clear, basting occasionally with remaining oil.

3. Meanwhile, in small saucepan, heat remaining cranberry sauce until melted. Remove hens from oven; remove and discard string. Spoon cranberry sauce over hens.

*Makes 4 servings*

# roast leg of lamb

**3 tablespoons coarse-grained mustard**
**2 cloves garlic, minced***
**1½ teaspoons dried rosemary, crushed**
**½ teaspoon black pepper**
**1 leg of lamb, well trimmed, boned, rolled and tied (about**
**4 pounds)**
**Mint jelly (optional)**

*For a more intense garlic flavor inside the meat, cut garlic into slivers. Cut small pockets at random intervals throughout roast with the tip of a sharp knife; insert the garlic slivers.*

1. Combine mustard, garlic, rosemary and pepper. Rub mustard mixture over lamb. Place roast on meat rack in foil-lined shallow roasting pan.** Preheat oven to 400°F. Roast 15 minutes. *Reduce oven temperature to 325°F;* roast about 20 minutes per pound for medium or until internal temperature reaches 145°F when tested with meat thermometer inserted into thickest part of roast.

2. Transfer roast to cutting board; cover with foil. Let stand 10 to 15 minutes before carving. Internal temperature will continue to rise 5° to 10°F during stand time.

3. Cut strings from roast; discard. Carve into 20 slices. Serve with mint jelly, if desired.                                                                    *Makes 10 servings*

**At this point the lamb may be covered and refrigerated up to 24 hours before roasting.*

# fancy swiss omelet roll

**1 cup milk**
**6 eggs**
**½ cup all-purpose flour**
**2 tablespoons butter or margarine, melted**
**½ teaspoon salt**
**¼ teaspoon white pepper**
**½ cup chopped roasted red pepper**
**2 ounces prosciutto or ham, thinly sliced and cut into strips**
**1 cup (4 ounces) shredded Swiss cheese**
**2 tablespoons chopped fresh basil**

1. Preheat oven to 350°F. Line bottom and sides of 15×10-inch jelly-roll pan with foil. Generously spray bottom and sides of foil with nonstick cooking spray.

2. Combine milk, eggs, flour, butter, salt and white pepper in medium bowl. Beat with electric mixer at medium speed until well blended. Pour into prepared pan. Bake 10 minutes. Sprinkle with red pepper and prosciutto.

3. Continue baking 8 to 10 minutes or until eggs are set, but not dry. Immediately sprinkle with cheese and basil.

4. Beginning with short end of omelet, carefully roll up omelet, using foil to gently lift omelet from pan.

5. To serve, transfer omelet roll to serving platter and cut into 1¼-inch-thick slices. Garnish, if desired. *Makes 4 servings*

fancy swiss omelet roll

# baked holiday ham with cranberry-wine compote

**2 teaspoons peanut oil**
**⅔ cup chopped onion**
**½ cup chopped celery**
**1 cup red wine**
**1 cup honey**
**½ cup sugar**
**1 package (12 ounces) fresh cranberries**
**1 fully-cooked smoked ham (10 pounds)**
**Whole cloves**
**Kumquats and currant leaves for garnish**

1. For Cranberry-Wine Compote, heat oil in large saucepan over medium-high heat until hot; add onion and celery. Cook until tender, stirring frequently. Stir in wine, honey and sugar; bring to a boil. Add cranberries; return to a boil. Reduce heat to low; cover and simmer 10 minutes. Cool completely.

2. Carefully ladle enough clear syrup from cranberry mixture into glass measuring cup to equal 1 cup; set aside. Transfer remaining cranberry mixture to small serving bowl; cover and refrigerate.

3. Slice away skin from ham with sharp utility knife. (Omit step if meat retailer has already removed skin.)

4. Preheat oven to 325°F. Score fat on ham in diamond design with sharp utility knife; stud with whole cloves. Place ham, fat side up, on rack in shallow roasting pan.

5. Bake, uncovered, 1½ hours. Baste ham with reserved cranberry-wine syrup. Bake 1 to 2 hours more or until meat thermometer inserted into thickest part of ham, not touching bone, registers 140°F, basting with cranberry-wine syrup twice.*

6. Let ham stand 10 minutes before transferring to warm serving platter. Slice ham with large carving knife. Serve warm with chilled Cranberry-Wine Compote. Garnish, if desired. *Makes 16 to 20 servings*

*Total cooking time for ham should be 18 to 24 minutes per pound.*

*baked holiday ham with cranberry-wine compote*

# roast turkey with cranberry stuffing

**1 loaf (12 ounces) Italian or French bread, cut into ½-inch cubes**
**2 tablespoons butter**
**1½ cups chopped onions**
**1½ cups chopped celery**
**2 teaspoons poultry seasoning**
**1 teaspoon dried thyme leaves**
**½ teaspoon dried rosemary, crushed**
**¼ teaspoon salt**
**¼ teaspoon black pepper**
**1 cup coarsely chopped fresh cranberries**
**1 tablespoon sugar**
**¾ cup chicken broth**
**1 turkey (8 to 10 pounds)**
**Fresh parsley sprigs (optional)**

1. Preheat oven to 375°F.

2. Arrange bread on two 15×10-inch jelly-roll pans. Bake 12 minutes or until lightly toasted. *Reduce oven temperature to 350°F.*

3. Melt butter in large saucepan over medium heat. Add onions and celery; cook and stir 8 minutes or until vegetables are tender; remove from heat. Add bread cubes, poultry seasoning, thyme, rosemary, salt and pepper; mix well. Combine cranberries and sugar in small bowl; mix well. Add to bread mixture; toss well. Drizzle chicken broth evenly over mixture; toss well.

4. Spray roasting pan and rack with nonstick cooking spray. Remove giblets from turkey. Rinse turkey and cavity in cold water; pat dry with paper towels. Fill turkey cavity loosely with stuffing. Place turkey, breast side up, on rack in roasting pan. Bake 3 hours or until thermometer inserted into thickest part of thigh registers 180°F and juices run clear.

5. Meanwhile, place remaining stuffing in casserole sprayed with nonstick cooking spray. Cover casserole; refrigerate until baking time.

6. Transfer turkey to serving platter. Cover loosely with foil; let stand 20 minutes. Place covered casserole of stuffing in oven; *increase temperature to 375°F.* Bake 25 to 30 minutes or until hot.

7. Remove and discard turkey skin. Slice turkey and serve with cranberry stuffing. Garnish with fresh parsley sprigs, if desired. *Makes 20 servings*

*roast turkey with cranberry stuffing*

# prime rib of beef a la lawry's®

**1 (8-pound) prime rib roast**
**3½ tablespoons LAWRY'S® Seasoned Salt**

Score fat on meat and rub generously with Seasoned Salt. Place prime rib on roasting rack in large roasting pan. Cook prime rib, uncovered, in preheated 325°F oven for 25 to 28 minutes per pound for medium rare or accelerate the cook time by cooking at 350°F for 18 to 22 minutes per pound. Remove roast from oven when internal temperature of roast reaches 125°F. Let stand 20 minutes before carving (internal temperature should rise to between 140° to 145°F).

*Makes 8 servings*

**MEAL IDEAS:** Garnish with watercress and spiced crab apples. Carve at tableside. Serve prime rib with horseradish.

**HINT:** To score fat, make shallow cuts in diamond pattern.

**Prep Time:** 5 minutes
**Cook Time:** varies with roast size (8-pound roast cooked rare to medium-rare takes 3 hours 20 minutes)

# rack of lamb with dijon-mustard sauce

**1 rack of lamb (3 pounds), all visible fat removed**
**1 cup finely chopped fresh parsley**
**½ cup Dijon mustard**
**½ cup soft whole wheat bread crumbs**
**1 tablespoon chopped fresh rosemary *or* 2 teaspoons dried rosemary**
**1 teaspoon minced garlic**
**Fresh rosemary, lemon slices and lemon peel strips for garnish (optional)**

Preheat oven to 500°F. Place lamb in large baking pan. Combine parsley, mustard, bread crumbs, rosemary and garlic in small bowl. Spread evenly over top of lamb. Place in center of oven; cook 7 minutes for medium-rare. Turn off oven but do not open door for 30 minutes. Garnish with additional fresh rosemary, lemon slices and lemon peel strips, if desired.

*Makes 6 servings*

# ham with cherry sauce

**5 pound fully cooked boneless ham**
**Whole cloves**

**Cherry Sauce**
**2 cans (16 ounces each) red tart pitted cherries in juice,**
**undrained (see Tip)**
**⅔ to ¾ cup unsweetened pineapple juice**
**1 tablespoon plus 1 teaspoon lemon juice**
**¼ cup cornstarch**
**1 to 1½ cups EQUAL® SPOONFUL***
**Red food coloring (optional)**
**Parsley sprigs**

*May substitute 24 packets EQUAL® sweetener.*

● Place ham in roasting pan; stud with cloves. Roast ham in preheated 325°F oven about 1½ hours or until thermometer inserted in center of ham registers 160°F.

● For Cherry Sauce, drain cherries, reserving juice in 2-cup glass measure. Add enough pineapple juice to make 2 cups. Pour juice mixture and lemon juice into medium saucepan; whisk in cornstarch until smooth.

● Heat to a boil, whisking constantly, about 1 minute. Add cherries to saucepan; cook over medium heat 3 to 4 minutes or until heated through. Stir in Equal® and food coloring, if desired. (Makes about 4⅔ cups sauce.)

● Slice ham and arrange on platter with bowl of Cherry Sauce in center. Garnish with parsley.                                  *Makes 16 servings*

**TIP:** Two packages (16 ounces each) frozen no-sugar-added pitted cherries, thawed, can be substituted for the canned cherries; drain cherries thoroughly and add enough pineapple juice to make 2 cups. Proceed with recipe as directed above.

# apple stuffed pork loin roast

**2 cloves garlic, minced**
**1 teaspoon coarse salt**
**1 teaspoon dried rosemary leaves**
**½ teaspoon dried thyme leaves**
**½ teaspoon freshly ground black pepper**
**1 boneless center cut pork loin roast (4 to 5 pounds)**
**1 tablespoon butter**
**2 large tart apples, peeled, cored and thinly sliced (2 cups)**
**1 medium onion, cut into thin strips (about 1 cup)**
**2 tablespoons brown sugar**
**1 teaspoon Dijon mustard**
**1 cup apple cider or apple juice**

1. Preheat oven to 325°F. Combine garlic, salt, rosemary, thyme and pepper in small bowl. Butterfly roast.* Rub half garlic mixture onto cut sides of pork.

2. Melt butter in large skillet over medium-high heat. Add apples and onion; cook and stir 5 to 10 minutes or until soft. Stir in brown sugar and mustard. Spread mixture evenly on one cut side of roast. Close halves; tie roast with cotton string at 2-inch intervals. Place roast on meat rack in shallow roasting pan. Pour apple juice over roast. Rub outside of roast with remaining garlic mixture.

3. Roast, uncovered, basting frequently with pan drippings, 2 to 2½ hours or until instant-read thermometer inserted into thickest part registers 155°F. Let roast stand for 15 minutes before slicing. The internal temperature will continue to rise 5° to 10°F during stand time. Carve roast crosswise.

*Makes 14 to 16 servings*

*Cut lengthwise down roast almost to, but not through, the bottom. Open like a book.*

*apple stuffed pork loin roast*

# roasted herb & garlic tenderloin

**1 beef tenderloin roast, trimmed (3 to 4 pounds)**
**1 tablespoon black peppercorns**
**2 tablespoons chopped fresh basil *or* 2 teaspoons dried basil leaves**
**4½ teaspoons chopped fresh thyme *or* 1½ teaspoons dried thyme leaves**
**1 tablespoon chopped fresh rosemary *or* 1 teaspoon dried rosemary**
**1 tablespoon minced garlic**
**Salt and black pepper (optional)**

1. Preheat oven to 425°F. To hold shape of roast, tie roast with cotton string at 1½-inch intervals. Place roast on meat rack in shallow roasting pan.

2. Place peppercorns in small heavy resealable plastic food storage bag. Squeeze out excess air; seal bag tightly. Pound peppercorns with flat side of meat mallet or rolling pin until peppercorns are cracked.

3. Combine cracked peppercorns, basil, thyme, rosemary and garlic in small bowl; rub over top surface of roast.

4. Roast 40 to 50 minutes until internal temperature reaches 135°F for medium rare or 150°F for medium when tested with meat thermometer inserted into thickest part of roast.

5. Transfer roast to cutting board; cover with foil. Let stand 10 to 15 minutes before carving. Internal temperature will continue to rise 5° to 10°F during stand time. Remove and discard string. To serve, carve crosswise into ½-inch-thick slices. Season with salt and pepper, if desired. *Makes 10 to 12 servings*

*roasted herb & garlic tenderloin*

# succulent roast turkey

**1 (12-pound) fresh or thawed frozen turkey**
**¼ cup (½ stick) butter, melted, divided**
**Salt, to taste**
**Freshly ground black pepper, to taste**
**1½ cups apple cider or apple juice**
**2 cups chicken broth, divided**
**Cider Pan Gravy (page 162)**

1. Preheat oven to 450°F. Rinse turkey in cold water; drain well and pat dry with paper towels. Stuff turkey, if desired.

2. Place on rack in large shallow roasting pan. Brush 2 tablespoons butter over turkey. Sprinkle salt and pepper lightly over turkey. Pour cider and 1 cup broth into bottom of roasting pan. Place in oven; roast 10 minutes. *Reduce oven temperature to 325°F* and continue roasting 1 hour. Brush remaining 2 tablespoons butter over turkey; add remaining 1 cup broth and continue roasting 1 hour. Baste turkey with pan juices; add additional broth if pan is dry to prevent drippings from burning. Continue baking until internal temperature of thigh meat registers 180°F and legs move easily in sockets, 30 minutes to 1 hour longer.

3. Transfer turkey to carving board or serving platter; tent with foil and let stand 20 to 30 minutes before carving. Reserve drippings* in roasting pan; prepare Cider Pan Gravy. Slice turkey; arrange on individual serving platters with gravy.

*Makes 10 to 12 servings*

*Drippings will be dark.*

*succulent roast turkey*

# inviting side dishes

## old-fashioned herb stuffing

**6 slices (8 ounces) whole wheat, rye or white bread (or combination), cut into ½-inch cubes**
**1 tablespoon butter**
**1 cup chopped onion**
**½ cup thinly sliced celery**
**½ cup thinly sliced carrot**
**1 cup canned chicken broth**
**1 tablespoon chopped fresh thyme _or_ 1 teaspoon dried thyme leaves**
**1 tablespoon chopped fresh sage _or_ 1 teaspoon dried sage leaves**
**½ teaspoon paprika**
**¼ teaspoon black pepper**

1. Preheat oven to 350°F. Place bread cubes on baking sheet; bake 10 minutes or until dry.

2. Melt butter in large saucepan over medium heat. Add onion, celery and carrot; cover and cook 10 minutes or until vegetables are tender. Add broth, thyme, sage, paprika and pepper; bring to a simmer. Stir in bread pieces; mix well. Remove pan from heat; set aside.

3. Coat 1½-quart baking dish with nonstick cooking spray. Spoon stuffing into dish. Cover and bake 25 to 30 minutes or until heated through.

_Makes 4 servings_

*old-fashioned herb stuffing*

# spicy pumpkin soup with green chili swirl

**1 can (4 ounces) diced green chilies**
**¼ cup sour cream**
**¼ cup fresh cilantro leaves**
**1 can (15 ounces) solid-pack pumpkin**
**1 can (14½ ounces) chicken broth**
**½ cup water**
**1 teaspoon ground cumin**
**½ teaspoon chili powder**
**¼ teaspoon garlic powder**
**⅛ teaspoon ground red pepper (optional)**
**Additional sour cream (optional)**

1. Combine chilies, ¼ cup sour cream and cilantro in food processor or blender; process until smooth.*

2. Combine pumpkin, broth, water, cumin, chili powder, garlic powder and red pepper, if desired, in medium saucepan; stir in ¼ cup green chili mixture. Bring to a boil; reduce heat to medium. Simmer, uncovered, 5 minutes, stirring occasionally.

3. Pour into serving bowls. Top each serving with small dollops of remaining green chili mixture and additional sour cream, if desired. Run tip of spoon through dollops to swirl.                                              *Makes 4 servings*

*Omit food processor step by adding green chilies directly to soup. Finely chop cilantro and combine with sour cream. Dollop with sour cream-cilantro mixture as directed.*

*spicy pumpkin soup with green chili swirl*

# festive cranberry mold

**½ cup water**
**1 package (6 ounces) raspberry-flavored gelatin**
**1 can (8 ounces) cranberry sauce**
**1⅔ cups cranberry juice cocktail**
**1 cup sliced bananas (optional)**
**½ cup walnuts, toasted (optional)**

1. Bring water to a boil in medium saucepan over medium-high heat. Add gelatin and stir until dissolved. Fold in cranberry sauce. Reduce heat to medium; cook until sauce is melted. Stir in cranberry juice cocktail.

2. Refrigerate mixture until slightly thickened. Fold in banana slices and walnuts, if desired. Pour mixture into 4-cup mold; cover and refrigerate until gelatin is set.

*Makes 8 servings*

# hot sweet potatoes

**4 small sweet potatoes (4 ounces each)**
**2 tablespoons margarine or unsalted butter, softened**
**½ teaspoon TABASCO® brand Pepper Sauce**
**¼ teaspoon dried savory leaves, crushed**

Cover potatoes with water in large saucepan. Cover and cook over high heat 20 to 25 minutes or until potatoes are tender. Drain potatoes and cut in half lengthwise.

Preheat broiler. Combine margarine and TABASCO® Sauce in small bowl. Spread ¾ teaspoon margarine mixture over cut side of each potato half. Season each with pinch of savory. Place on foil-lined broiler pan and broil, watching carefully, about 5 minutes or until lightly browned. Serve hot. *Makes 4 servings*

*festive cranberry mold*

# cranberry bread pudding

**1 quart whole milk or reduced-fat (2%)**
**2 cups granulated sugar**
**5 large eggs _or_ 1¼ cups egg substitute**
**1 cup dried sweetened cranberries**
**2 tablespoons vanilla**
**1 tablespoon baking powder**
**½ teaspoon ground cinnamon**
**1 loaf (16 ounces) French bread, torn into small pieces**

**Brandy Sauce**
**1½ cups granulated sugar**
**1 cup (2 sticks) butter**
**½ cup whole milk or reduced-fat (2%)**
**½ to ¾ cup brandy**

1. Preheat oven to 350°F. Spray 13×9-inch baking dish with nonstick cooking spray. Combine 1 quart milk, 2 cups sugar, eggs, cranberries, vanilla, baking powder and cinnamon in large bowl; stir until well blended. Add bread and toss to blend thoroughly. Pour mixture into prepared dish. Bake 50 to 70 minutes or until golden and knife inserted into center comes out clean.

2. To make Brandy Sauce, combine 1½ cups sugar with butter and ½ cup milk in small saucepan. Heat over medium-high heat, stirring frequently, until sugar dissolves. Remove from heat. Stir in brandy.

3. Cut bread pudding into 12 squares and place on individual dessert plates. Spoon ¼ cup sauce over each serving. _Makes 12 servings_

# sherried mushrooms

**½ cup (1 stick) butter**
**1 cup HOLLAND HOUSE® Sherry Cooking Wine**
**1 clove garlic, crushed**
**18 fresh mushrooms, sliced**
**Salt and black pepper**

Melt butter in medium skillet over medium heat. Add cooking wine and garlic. Add mushrooms; cook until tender, about 5 minutes, stirring frequently. Season to taste with salt and pepper. _Makes 2 to 3 servings_

# polenta triangles

**½ cup yellow corn grits**
**1 ½ cups chicken broth, divided**
**2 cloves garlic, minced**
**½ cup (2 ounces) crumbled feta cheese**
**1 red bell pepper, roasted,\* peeled and finely chopped**
**Nonstick cooking spray**

*\*Place pepper on foil-lined broiler pan; broil 15 minutes or until blackened on all sides, turning every 5 minutes. Place bell pepper in paper bag; close bag and let stand 15 minutes before peeling.*

1. Combine grits and ½ cup broth; mix well. Set aside.

2. Pour remaining 1 cup broth into large heavy saucepan; bring to a boil. Add garlic and moistened grits; mix well and return to a boil. Reduce heat to low; cover and cook 20 minutes. Remove from heat; add feta cheese. Stir until cheese is completely melted. Add bell pepper; mix well.

3. Spray 8-inch square baking pan with cooking spray. Spoon grits mixture into prepared pan. Press grits evenly into pan. Refrigerate until cold.

4. Preheat broiler. Turn polenta out onto cutting board; cut into 2-inch squares. Cut each square diagonally into 2 triangles. Spray baking sheet with cooking spray. Place polenta triangles on prepared baking sheet; spray tops lightly with cooking spray. Place under broiler until lightly browned. Turn triangles over and broil until browned and crisp. Serve warm or at room temperature. Garnish with fresh oregano and chives, if desired. *Makes 6 to 8 servings*

# apple pecan stuffing

**½ cup (1 stick) butter**
**1 large onion, chopped**
**1 large Granny Smith apple, peeled, diced**
**2½ cups chicken broth**
**1 package (16 ounces) cornbread stuffing mix**
**½ cup chopped pecans, toasted**

1. Preheat oven to 325°F. Melt butter in large saucepan. Add onion; cook 5 minutes, stirring occasionally. Add apple; cook 1 minute. Add broth; bring to a simmer. Remove from heat; stir in stuffing mix and pecans.

2. Place stuffing in an ovenproof casserole dish. Cover; bake in 325°F oven for 45 minutes or until hot.                    *Makes 10 to 12 servings*

**NOTE:** Stuffing may be prepared up to 1 day before serving (store covered and refrigerated). Let stand at room temperature 30 minutes before baking.

*apple pecan stuffing*

# glazed maple acorn squash

**1 large acorn or golden acorn squash**
**¼ cup water**
**2 tablespoons pure maple syrup**
**1 tablespoon butter, melted**
**¼ teaspoon ground cinnamon**

1. Preheat oven to 375°F.

2. Cut stem and blossom ends from squash. Cut squash crosswise into five equal slices. Discard seeds and membrane. Place water in 13×9-inch baking dish. Arrange squash in dish; cover with foil. Bake 30 minutes or until tender.

3. Combine syrup, butter and cinnamon in small bowl; mix well. Uncover squash; pour off water. Brush squash with syrup mixture, letting excess pool in center of squash.

4. Return to oven; bake 10 minutes or until syrup mixture is bubbly.

*Makes 5 servings*


# baked apples

**2 tablespoons sugar**
**2 tablespoons raisins, chopped**
**2 tablespoons chopped walnuts**
**2 tablespoons GRANDMA'S® Molasses**
**6 apples, cored**

Heat oven to 350°F. In medium bowl, combine sugar, raisins, walnuts and molasses. Fill apple cavities with molasses mixture. Place in 13×9-inch baking dish. Pour ½ cup hot water over apples and bake 25 minutes or until soft.

*Makes 6 servings*

glazed maple acorn squash

# wild rice with dried apricots and cranberries

**½ cup uncooked wild rice**
**3 cups chicken broth, divided**
**1 cup apple juice**
**¾ cup uncooked long-grain white rice**
**½ cup golden raisins**
**½ cup chopped dried apricots**
**½ cup dried cranberries**
**2 tablespoons butter**
**¾ cup chopped onion**
**½ cup coarsely chopped pecans**
**⅓ cup chopped fresh parsley**
**Fresh rosemary sprigs, orange slices and whole cranberries for garnish (optional)**

1. Rinse wild rice in fine strainer under cold running water. Drain.

2. Combine wild rice, 1½ cups chicken broth and apple juice in large saucepan. Bring to a boil over medium-high heat. Reduce heat to low; simmer, covered, about 45 minutes or until rice is tender. Drain.

3. Combine white rice and remaining 1½ cups broth in separate large saucepan. Bring to a boil over medium-high heat. Reduce heat to low; simmer, covered, 12 to 15 minutes.

4. Stir in raisins, apricots and cranberries; simmer 5 minutes or until rice is tender, fluffy and liquid is absorbed. Remove from heat. Let stand, covered, 5 minutes or until fruit is tender; set aside.

5. Melt butter in large skillet over medium heat. Add onion; cook and stir 5 to 6 minutes or until tender. Stir in pecans. Cook and stir 2 minutes.

6. Add wild rice and white rice mixtures to skillet. Stir in parsley; cook and stir over medium heat about 2 minutes or until heated through. Garnish with fresh rosemary, orange slices and whole cranberries, if desired.

*Makes 6 to 8 servings*

*wild rice with dried apricots and cranberries*

# orange-spice glazed carrots

**1 package (32 ounces) baby carrots**
**½ cup packed light brown sugar**
**½ cup orange juice**
**3 tablespoons butter**
**¾ teaspoon ground cinnamon**
**¼ teaspoon ground nutmeg**
**2 tablespoons cornstarch**
**¼ cup cold water**

## Slow Cooker Directions

Combine all ingredients except cornstarch and water in slow cooker. Cover; cook on LOW 3½ to 4 hours or until carrots are crisp-tender. Spoon carrots into serving bowl. Remove juices to small saucepan. Heat to a boil. Mix cornstarch and water in small bowl until blended. Stir into saucepan. Boil 1 minute or until thickened, stirring constantly. Spoon over carrots. *Makes 6 servings*

# turkey-tomato soup

**2 medium turkey thighs, boned, skinned and cut into 1-inch pieces**
**1¾ cups chicken broth**
**1½ cups frozen corn**
**2 small white or red potatoes, cubed**
**1 cup chopped onion**
**1 cup water**
**1 can (8 ounces) tomato sauce**
**¼ cup tomato paste**
**2 tablespoons Dijon mustard**
**1 teaspoon hot pepper sauce**
**½ teaspoon sugar**
**½ teaspoon garlic powder**
**¼ cup finely chopped fresh parsley**

## Slow Cooker Directions

Combine all ingredients, except parsley, in slow cooker. Cover; cook on LOW 9 to 10 hours. Stir in parsley; serve. *Makes 6 servings*

# christmas cabbage slaw

**2 cups finely shredded green cabbage**
**2 cups finely shredded red cabbage**
**1 cup jicama strips**
**¼ cup diced green bell pepper**
**¼ cup thinly sliced green onions with tops**
**¼ cup vegetable oil**
**¼ cup lime juice**
**¾ teaspoon salt**
**⅛ teaspoon black pepper**
**2 tablespoons coarsely chopped fresh cilantro**

Combine cabbages, jícama, bell pepper and onions in large bowl. Whisk oil, lime juice, salt and black pepper in small bowl until well blended. Stir in cilantro. Pour over cabbage mixture; toss lightly. Cover; refrigerate 2 to 6 hours for flavors to blend.                                                   *Makes 4 to 6 servings*

# sweet potato puffs

**2 pounds sweet potatoes**
**⅓ cup orange juice**
**1 egg, beaten**
**1 tablespoon grated orange peel**
**½ teaspoon ground nutmeg**
**¼ cup chopped pecans**

1. Peel and cut sweet potatoes into 1-inch pieces. Place potatoes in medium saucepan. Add enough water to cover; bring to a boil over medium-high heat. Cook 10 to 15 minutes or until tender. Drain potatoes and place in large bowl; mash until smooth. Add orange juice, egg, orange peel and nutmeg; mix well.

2. Preheat oven to 375°F. Spray baking sheet with nonstick cooking spray. Spoon potato mixture into 10 mounds on prepared baking sheet. Sprinkle pecans on tops of mounds.

3. Bake 30 minutes or until centers are hot. Garnish, if desired.
                                                   *Makes 10 servings*

# butternut bisque

**1 teaspoon butter**
**1 large onion, coarsely chopped**
**1 medium butternut squash (about 1½ pounds), peeled, seeded
and cut into ½-inch pieces**
**2 cans (about 14 ounces each) chicken broth, divided**
**½ teaspoon ground nutmeg or freshly grated nutmeg**
**⅛ teaspoon white pepper**
**Plain nonfat yogurt and chives for garnish (optional)**

1. Melt butter in large saucepan over medium heat. Add onion; cook and stir 3 minutes.

2. Add squash and 1 can chicken broth; bring to a boil over high heat. Reduce heat to low; cover and simmer 20 minutes or until squash is very tender.

3. Process squash mixture, in 2 batches, in food processor until smooth. Return soup to saucepan; add remaining can of broth, nutmeg and pepper. Simmer, uncovered, 5 minutes, stirring occasionally.*

4. Ladle soup into soup bowls. Place yogurt in pastry bag fitted with round decorating tip. Pipe onto soup in decorative design. Garnish with chives, if desired.

*Makes 6 servings (about 5 cups)*

*At this point, soup may be covered and refrigerated up to 2 days before serving. Reheat over medium heat, stirring occasionally.*

**CREAM OF BUTTERNUT SOUP:** Add ½ cup whipping cream or half-and-half with second can of broth. Proceed as directed.

*butternut bisque*

# asparagus wreath

**1 pound fresh asparagus, ends trimmed**
**1 tablespoon butter**
**1 teaspoon lemon juice**
**6 thin slices pepperoni, finely chopped**
**¼ cup seasoned dry bread crumbs**
**Pimiento strips for garnish**

1. Peel asparagus stalks, if desired. Steam asparagus in large covered saucepan 5 to 8 minutes or until crisp-tender.

2. Arrange asparagus in wreath shape on warm, round serving platter.

3. Heat butter and lemon juice in small saucepan until butter is melted; pour over asparagus. Combine chopped pepperoni and bread crumbs in small bowl; sprinkle over asparagus. Garnish, if desired. *Makes 4 side-dish servings*

# waldorf salad

**1 unpeeled tart red apple, such as McIntosh, coarsely chopped**
**1 teaspoon fresh lemon juice**
**4 teaspoons frozen apple juice concentrate, thawed**
**1 tablespoon mayonnaise**
**1 tablespoon sour cream**
**⅛ teaspoon paprika**
**½ cup finely chopped celery**
**6 large lettuce leaves, washed**
**5 teaspoons coarsely chopped walnuts**

1. Combine apple and lemon juice in resealable plastic food storage bag. Seal bag; toss to coat.

2. Combine apple juice concentrate, mayonnaise, sour cream and paprika in medium bowl until well blended. Add apple mixture and celery; toss to coat. Cover; refrigerate 2 hours before serving.

3. Serve each salad over lettuce leaves. Top each serving evenly with walnuts. *Makes 2 servings*

*asparagus wreath*

# green beans with blue cheese and roasted peppers

**1 bag (20 ounces) frozen cut green beans**
**½ jar (about 3 ounces) roasted red pepper strips, drained and slivered**
**⅛ teaspoon salt**
**⅛ teaspoon white pepper**
**4 ounces cream cheese**
**½ cup milk**
**¾ cup blue cheese (3 ounces), crumbled**
**½ cup Italian-style bread crumbs**
**1 tablespoon butter, melted**

1. Preheat oven to 350°F. Spray 2-quart oval casserole with nonstick cooking spray.

2. Combine green beans, red pepper strips, salt and white pepper in prepared dish.

3. Place cream cheese and milk in small saucepan; heat over low heat, stirring until melted. Add blue cheese; stir only until combined. Pour cheese mixture over green bean mixture and stir until green beans are coated.

4. Combine bread crumbs and butter in small bowl; sprinkle evenly over casserole.

5. Bake, uncovered, 20 minutes or until hot and bubbly.          *Makes 4 servings*

*green beans with blue cheese and roasted peppers*

# fresh cranberry salad

**1 cup water**
**3 cups fresh cranberries**
**3 packets sucralose no-calorie sugar substitute**
**1 package (4-serving size) raspberry-flavored gelatin**
**¾ cup cold water**
**½ cup peeled, diced orange**
**½ cup diced celery**
**1 tablespoon finely grated orange zest**

1. Bring water to a boil in medium saucepan over medium-high heat. Add cranberries and sugar substitute. Cook and stir until mixture returns to a boil. Reduce heat to medium and simmer, stirring occasionally, 10 minutes or until cranberries have popped open. Mixture will be thick.

2. Pour gelatin into medium heat-safe bowl. Pour hot cranberry mixture over gelatin and stir until gelatin dissolves completely.

3. Stir in cold water, diced orange, celery and orange zest. Mix well; pour into 8-inch square pan and refrigerate until set, about 4 hours.       *Makes 8 servings*

# sour cream garlic mashed potatoes

**2 pounds red potatoes, peeled\* and cut into 1-inch chunks**
**6 cloves garlic, peeled**
**¼ cup (½ stick) butter**
**1 cup sour cream**
**1 teaspoon salt, or to taste**
**½ teaspoon white pepper**

*\*For more texture, you may prefer to leave the potatoes unpeeled.*

Place potatoes and garlic in large saucepan; cover with water. Bring to a boil over high heat. Reduce heat; simmer about 20 minutes or until potatoes are tender. Drain well in colander; return to saucepan. Add butter; mash potatoes. Stir in sour cream, salt and pepper.       *Makes 8 to 10 servings*

# sweet potato gratin

**3 pounds sweet potatoes (about 5 large)**
**½ cup (1 stick) butter, divided**
**¼ cup plus 2 tablespoons packed light brown sugar, divided**
**2 eggs**
**⅔ cup orange juice**
**2 teaspoons ground cinnamon, divided**
**½ teaspoon salt**
**¼ teaspoon ground nutmeg**
**⅓ cup all-purpose flour**
**¼ cup uncooked old-fashioned oats**
**⅓ cup chopped pecans or walnuts**

1. Preheat oven to 350°F. Bake sweet potatoes about 1 hour or until tender.*

2. Cut hot sweet potatoes lengthwise into halves. Scrape hot pulp from skins into large bowl; discard skins.

3. Beat ¼ cup butter and 2 tablespoons sugar into sweet potatoes with electric mixer at medium speed until butter is melted. Add eggs, orange juice, 1½ teaspoons cinnamon, salt and nutmeg. Beat until smooth. Pour mixture into 1½-quart baking dish or gratin dish; smooth top.

4. For topping, combine flour, oats, remaining ¼ cup sugar and remaining ½ teaspoon cinnamon in medium bowl. Cut in remaining ¼ cup butter until mixture resembles coarse crumbs. Stir in pecans. Sprinkle topping evenly over sweet potatoes.**

5. Bake 25 to 30 minutes or until sweet potatoes are heated through. For crisper topping, broil 5 inches from heat 2 to 3 minutes or until golden brown.

*Makes 6 to 8 servings*

*You may also pierce sweet potatoes several times with table fork and place on microwavable plate. Microwave at HIGH 16 to 18 minutes, rotating and turning potatoes over after 9 minutes. Let stand 5 minutes.*

**At this point, Sweet Potato Gratin may be covered and refrigerated up to 1 day. Let stand at room temperature 1 hour before baking.*

# delicious corn soufflé

**3 eggs**
**3 tablespoons all-purpose flour**
**1 tablespoon sugar**
**½ teaspoon black pepper**
**1 can (16½ ounces) cream-style corn**
**2 cups frozen corn kernels, thawed and drained**
**1 cup (4 ounces) shredded Mexican cheese blend**
**1 jar (2 ounces) pimientos, drained and diced**
**⅓ cup milk**
**Sprigs of fresh parsley (optional)**

1. Preheat oven to 350°F. Spray 8-inch round baking dish with nonstick cooking spray; place in oven.

2. Combine eggs, flour, sugar and pepper in large bowl; beat with electric mixer at high speed until smooth. Stir in cream-style corn, corn kernels, cheese, pimientos and milk. Pour into hot baking dish.

3. Bake, uncovered, 55 minutes or until set. Let stand 15 minutes before serving. Garnish with parsley, if desired. *Makes 6 servings*

# roasted sweet potatoes with cinnamon & sweet onions

**2 pounds sweet potatoes, peeled**
**1 sweet onion, cut into eighths**
**2 cloves garlic, chopped**
**¼ cup olive oil**
**½ teaspoon ground cinnamon**
**2 tablespoons orange juice**
**Salt and black pepper**

1. Preheat oven to 400°F. Cut potatoes in half lengthwise, then into 1-inch thick slices.

2. Place potatoes, onion and garlic in 12×8-inch baking dish.

3. Combine olive oil and cinnamon. Pour over potato mixture. Sprinkle with orange juice, salt and pepper; toss until well coated.

4. Cover with foil; bake 35 to 40 minutes or until potatoes are tender.
*Makes 6 servings*

*delicious corn soufflé*

# fruited wild rice with toasted nuts

**2 boxes (6.2 ounces each) fast-cooking long-grain and wild rice**
**2 tablespoons walnut or vegetable oil, divided**
**1 package (2½ ounces) walnut pieces *or* ⅔ cup slivered almonds**
**1 package (2¼ ounces) pecan pieces**
**2 cups chopped onions**
**12 dried apricots, sliced (about ½ cup)**
**½ cup dried cherries or cranberries**
**2 teaspoons minced fresh ginger**
**¼ teaspoon red pepper flakes**
**¼ cup honey**
**3 tablespoons soy sauce**
**1 tablespoon grated orange peel**

1. Cook rice according to package directions.

2. Meanwhile, heat 1 tablespoon oil in large nonstick skillet or wok over medium-high heat 1 minute. Add walnuts and pecans; cook, stirring frequently, 8 minutes or until pecans are browned. Remove from skillet and set aside.

3. Add remaining 1 tablespoon oil and onions to skillet; cook 10 minutes or until onions begin to brown. Add apricots, cherries, ginger, red pepper flakes and reserved nuts; cook 5 minutes.

4. Whisk together honey, soy sauce and orange peel in small bowl; add to onion mixture. Toss with rice. *Makes 4 servings*

**NOTE:** This dish can be served as a chilled rice salad. Spoon hot cooked rice evenly on large baking sheet to cool quickly, about 8 to 10 minutes. Toss with cooled nuts, onion mixture and honey mixture.

*fruited wild rice with toasted nuts*

# cornbread stuffing with sausage and apple

**⅓ cup pecan pieces**
**1 pound bulk pork sausage**
**1 large Jonathan apple**
**1⅓ cups chicken broth**
**¼ cup apple juice**
**6 ounces seasoned cornbread stuffing mix**

1. Preheat oven to 300°F. Place pecan pieces in shallow baking pan. Bake 6 to 8 minutes or until lightly browned, stirring frequently.

2. Place sausage in large skillet; cook over high heat 10 minutes or until meat is no longer pink, breaking meat apart with wooden spoon. Pour off drippings.

3. Meanwhile, coarsely chop apple. Place in large saucepan. Add broth, apple juice and seasoning packet from stuffing mix. Bring to a boil, uncovered, over high heat. Remove from heat; stir in stuffing mix. Cover; let stand 3 to 5 minutes or until stuffing is moist and tender.

4. Stir sausage into stuffing. Top with nuts. *Makes 4 servings*

# candied pineapple yams

**5 pounds yams or sweet potatoes, washed and pierced with fork**
**½ cup DOLE® Pineapple Juice**
**¼ cup (½ stick) margarine, melted**
**½ teaspoon salt**
**½ teaspoon pumpkin pie spice**
**½ cup packed brown sugar**
**1 container (16 ounces) DOLE® Fresh Pineapple, cut into slices**

● Place yams on foil-lined baking sheet. Bake at 350°F, 90 minutes or until yams are tender when pricked with fork.

● Spoon out baked yams from skins and place into large mixing bowl. Add pineapple juice, margarine, salt and pumpkin pie spice. Beat until fluffy.

● Spoon mixture into lightly greased 13×9-inch baking dish. Sprinkle with brown sugar. Arrange pineapple slices over yams. Continue baking at 350°F, 15 minutes or until hot. Garnish with fresh rosemary, if desired. Serve with roasted pork tenderloin and green peas. *Makes 10 servings*

*cornbread stuffing with sausage and apple*

# santa's favorite cookies

## chocolate-raspberry kolacky

2 squares (1 ounce each) semisweet chocolate, coarsely chopped
1½ cups all-purpose flour
¼ teaspoon baking soda
¼ teaspoon salt
½ cup (1 stick) butter, softened
3 ounces cream cheese or light cream cheese, softened
⅓ cup granulated sugar
1 teaspoon vanilla
   Seedless raspberry jam
   Powdered sugar

1. Place chocolate in small microwavable bowl. Microwave at HIGH 1 to 1½ minutes or until chocolate is melted, stirring after 1 minute. Let cool slightly.

2. Combine flour, baking soda and salt in small bowl; stir well. Beat butter and cream cheese in large bowl with electric mixer at medium speed until well blended. Beat in granulated sugar until light and fluffy. Beat in vanilla and melted chocolate. Gradually add flour mixture. Beat at low speed just until blended. Divide dough in half; flatten each half into disc. Wrap separately in plastic wrap. Refrigerate 1 to 2 hours or until firm.

3. Preheat oven to 375°F. Lightly grease cookie sheets. Roll out each dough disc on well-floured surface to ¼- to ⅛-inch thickness. Cut dough with 3-inch round cookie cutter. Place cutouts 2 inches apart on prepared cookie sheets. Place rounded ½ teaspoon jam in center of each circle. Bring three edges of dough circles up over jam; pinch edges together to seal, leaving center of triangle slightly open.

4. Bake 10 minutes or until set. Let cookies stand on cookie sheets 2 minutes. Remove cookies to wire racks; cool completely. Just before serving, sprinkle with powdered sugar. Store tightly covered in refrigerator; let stand 30 minutes at room temperature before serving.          *Makes about 1½ dozen cookies*

NOTE: These cookies do not freeze well.

CHOCOLATE-RASPBERRY KOLACKY CUPS: Fit dough circles into greased mini-muffin cups; fill with heaping teaspoonful jam. Bake 10 minutes or until set. Let pans stand on wire racks; cool completely. Dust with powdered sugar before serving.

*chocolate-raspberry kolacky*

# toasted almond and cranberry biscotti

**4 tablespoons butter, softened, divided**
**1 cup whole blanched almonds**
**2½ cups all-purpose flour**
**1 cup granulated sugar**
**1 teaspoon baking powder**
**½ teaspoon baking soda**
**2 eggs**
**1 teaspoon almond extract**
**¼ teaspoon vanilla**
**½ cup milk**
**1 cup dried cranberries**
**2 tablespoons packed brown sugar**

1. Preheat oven to 350°F. Lightly grease cookie sheets.

2. Melt 1 tablespoon butter in small skillet. Remove from heat; add almonds. Stir gently to coat almonds. Place in single layer on *ungreased* baking pan. Bake 8 to 10 minutes or until golden brown and fragrant, stirring frequently. Almonds can easily burn so watch carefully. Immediately remove almonds from pan; cool completely.

3. Stir together flour, sugar, baking powder and baking soda in large bowl. Add eggs, almond extract, vanilla and 2 tablespoons butter; beat with electric mixer at medium-low speed until soft dough forms. Continue beating adding only enough milk, 1 tablespoon at a time, to make smooth dough. Add almonds and cranberries. Knead dough gently in bowl until well blended. Transfer dough to floured surface; divide in half. Shape each half into 12×2-inch loaf on prepared cookie sheet.

4. Bake about 15 minutes or until lightly browned on top. Remove from oven and roll logs over exposing unbrowned bottoms. Return to oven; bake 15 minutes more or until evenly browned all over (loaf will sound hollow when tapped). Cool on wire rack 12 to 15 minutes or until cool enough to handle with bare hands.

5. While still warm, slice diagonally into pieces about ½ inch thick. Place slices on *ungreased* cookie sheets. Bake 10 minutes more on each side or until brown. Remove to wire racks; cool completely.

6. Melt remaining 1 tablespoon butter with brown sugar in small skillet over medium-high heat. Cook and stir until dark golden brown. Drizzle in thin ribbons over cooling cookies. *Makes about 4 dozen cookies*

*toasted almond and cranberry biscotti*

# sweet leaf wreath

**Gingerbread Cookie Dough (page 222)**
**Chocolate Leaves (recipe follows)**
**1 cup powdered sugar**
**1 egg white***
**Red cinnamon candies**

**Supplies**
**1 (8-inch) cardboard circle**
**Red ribbon bow**

*Use only grade A clean, uncracked eggs.

1. Prepare Gingerbread Cookie Dough. Prepare Chocolate Leaves using semisweet chocolate only; set aside.

2. Preheat oven to 350°F. Grease cookie sheets. Roll dough on floured surface to ⅛-inch thickness. Using 3½-inch cookie cutters, cut out 8 holly leaves and 8 rounded leaves. Mark veins in leaves with tip of knife. Bake 8 to 10 minutes until edges begin to brown. Remove to wire racks; cool completely.

3. Cut center out of cardboard circle, leaving 2-inch-wide ring. Cover ring with foil. Arrange cookies on cardboard ring.

4. Beat egg white and powdered sugar in small bowl. Use frosting to attach leaves to cardboard ring and to each other.** Decorate with red cinnamon candies, Chocolate Leaves and bow, attaching with frosting.     *Makes 1 wreath*

**To prevent frosting from drying, keep bowl of frosting covered with damp towel while working.

# chocolate leaves

**¾ cup coarsely chopped white chocolate baking bars**
**Red food coloring**
**Shortening**
**¾ cup coarsely chopped semisweet chocolate**

**Supplies**
**6 to 8 medium and 4 or 5 large lemon leaves***
**Pastry brush**

*These non-toxic leaves are available in florist shops.

*continued on page 222*

*sweet leaf wreath*

*sweet leaf wreath,* continued

1. Melt white chocolate in top of double boiler over hot, not boiling water, stirring constantly. Stir in red food coloring, a few drops at a time, until desired shade is reached. If chocolate begins to thicken or loses its shine, stir in shortening, 1 teaspoon at a time until smooth.

2. Brush thin layer of pink chocolate on back side of each medium-sized leaf with pastry brush. Do not spread to edge of leaf. Place on waxed paper-lined baking sheet. Refrigerate about 30 minutes or until firm.

3. Repeat with semisweet chocolate and large leaves. Refrigerate about 30 minutes or until firm.

4. Gently peel chocolate off leaves, beginning at stem ends. Refrigerate until ready to use.

# gingerbread cookie dough

**½ cup shortening**
**⅓ cup packed light brown sugar**
**¼ cup dark molasses**
**1 egg white**
**½ teaspoon vanilla**
**1½ cups all-purpose flour**
**1 teaspoon ground cinnamon**
**½ teaspoon baking soda**
**½ teaspoon salt**
**½ teaspoon ground ginger**
**¼ teaspoon baking powder**

1. Beat shortening, brown sugar, molasses, egg white and vanilla in large bowl with electric mixer at high speed until smooth.

2. Combine flour, cinnamon, baking soda, salt, ginger and baking powder in small bowl. Add to shortening mixture; mix well. Cover; refrigerate about 8 hours or until firm.

# storefront place cards

**1 recipe Gingerbread Cookie Dough (page 222)**
**Powdered sugar**
**Cookie Glaze (recipe follows)**
**Assorted food colorings and candies**

**Supplies**
**Pastry bags and small writing tips**

1. Preheat oven to 350°F. On floured surface, roll dough to ¼-inch thickness. Cut out 16 to 20 (4×3-inch) rectangles. Place 2 inches apart on ungreased cookie sheets. Bake 12 to 14 minutes or until edges begin to brown. Remove to wire racks; cool completely.

2. Prepare Cookie Glaze, adding 2 to 3 tablespoons additional powdered sugar to glaze; divide into separate bowls for each color of frosting desired. Tint with food colorings as desired. Spoon into pastry bags fitted with writing tips. Pipe designs and names onto half of cookies. Decorate with candies to look like holiday storefronts or houses, using glaze to attach candies. Let stand until glaze is set.

3. To assemble place cards, spread some remaining glaze on top edges of undecorated cookies; press to backs of decorated cookies at top. Separate bottoms so cookies make upside-down "V," and cookies can stand without support (see picture on page 251). Let stand until glaze is set.    *Makes 8 to 10 place cards*

**COOKIE GLAZE:** Combine 4 cups powdered sugar and ¼ cup milk in small bowl; stir. Add 1 to 2 tablespoons additional milk as needed to make medium-thick, pourable glaze.

# orange-almond sables

**1½ cups powdered sugar**
**1 cup (2 sticks) butter, softened**
**1 tablespoon finely grated orange peel**
**1 tablespoon almond-flavored liqueur *or* 1 teaspoon almond extract**
**¾ cup whole blanched almonds, toasted***
**1¾ cups all-purpose flour**
**¼ teaspoon salt**
**1 egg, beaten**

*\* To toast almonds, spread in single layer on baking sheet. Bake in preheated 350°F oven 8 to 10 minutes or until brown, stirring twice.*

1. Preheat oven to 375°F.

2. Beat powdered sugar and butter in large bowl with electric mixer at medium speed until light and fluffy. Beat in orange peel and liqueur.

3. Reserve 24 whole almonds. Place remaining cooled almonds in food processor. Process using on/off pulsing action until almonds are ground, but not pasty.

4. Combine ground almonds, flour and salt in medium bowl; stir. Gradually add to butter mixture. Beat with electric mixer at low speed until well blended.

5. Roll dough on lightly floured surface with lightly floured rolling pin to just under ¼-inch thickness. Cut dough with floured 2½-inch round or fluted cookie cutter. Place cutouts 2 inches apart on ungreased cookie sheets.

6. Lightly brush tops of cutouts with beaten egg. Press one whole reserved almond in center of each cutout. Brush almond lightly with beaten egg. Bake 10 to 12 minutes or until light golden brown.

7. Let cookies stand 1 minute on cookie sheets. Remove cookies with spatula to wire racks; cool completely. Store tightly covered at room temperature, or freeze up to 3 months.

*Makes about 2 dozen cookies*

*orange-almond sables*

# cranberry-lime squares

**2¼ cups all-purpose flour, divided**
**½ cup powdered sugar**
**1 tablespoon plus 1 teaspoon grated lime peel**
**¼ teaspoon salt**
**1 cup (2 sticks) unsalted butter**
**2 cups granulated sugar**
**1 teaspoon baking powder**
**4 eggs**
**¼ cup lime juice (about 1½ limes)**
**1 cup dried cranberries**
**Additional powdered sugar**

1. Preheat oven to 350°F. Grease 13×9-inch baking pan. Combine 2 cups flour, powdered sugar, 1 tablespoon lime peel and salt in medium bowl. Cut in butter with pastry blender or two knives until mixture forms coarse crumbs. Press mixture evenly into baking pan. Bake 18 to 20 minutes or until golden brown.

2. Meanwhile, combine remaining ¼ cup flour, granulated sugar and baking powder. In separate bowl, combine eggs and lime juice. Add flour mixture to egg mixture beating well with electric mixer at medium speed. Stir in remaining 1 teaspoon lime peel and cranberries. Pour over warm crust; bake 20 to 25 minutes or until golden brown and set. Cool completely on wire rack. Sprinkle with powdered sugar; chill two hours. Cut into squares. Serve chilled.

*Makes 35 squares*

*cranberry-lime squares*

# holiday mini kisses treasure cookies

**1½ cups graham cracker crumbs**
**½ cup all-purpose flour**
**2 teaspoons baking powder**
**1 can (14 ounces) sweetened condensed milk (not evaporated milk)**
**½ cup (1 stick) butter, softened**
**1¾ cups (10-ounce package) HERSHEY'S MINI KISSES® Milk Chocolates**
**1⅓ cups candy-coated chocolate pieces**
**1⅓ cups MOUNDS® Sweetened Coconut Flakes**
**1 cup coarsely chopped walnuts**

1. Heat oven to 375°F. Stir together graham cracker crumbs, flour and baking powder in small bowl; set aside.

2. Beat sweetened condensed milk and butter until smooth; add reserved crumb mixture, mixing well. Stir in chocolate pieces, candy-coated chocolate pieces, coconut and walnuts. Drop by rounded tablespoons onto ungreased cookie sheet.

3. Bake 8 to 10 minutes or until lightly browned. Cool 1 minute; remove from cookie sheet to wire rack. Cool completely.          *Makes about 3 dozen cookies*

# thumbprints

**1 package (20 ounces) refrigerated sugar or chocolate cookie dough**
**All-purpose flour (optional)**
**¾ cup plus 1 tablespoon fruit preserves, any flavor**

1. Grease cookie sheets. Remove dough from wrapper according to package directions. Sprinkle with flour to minimize sticking, if necessary.

2. Cut dough into 26 (1-inch) slices; shape into balls, sprinkling with additional flour, if necessary. Place balls 2 inches apart on prepared cookie sheets. Press deep indentation in center of each ball with thumb. Freeze dough 20 minutes.

3. Preheat oven to 350°F. Bake cookies 12 to 13 minutes or until edges are light golden brown (cookies will have started to puff up and lose their shape). Quickly press down indentation using tip of teaspoon.

4. Return to oven 2 to 3 minutes or until cookies are golden brown and set. Cool cookies completely on cookie sheets. Fill each indentation with about 1½ teaspoons preserves.          *Makes 26 cookies*

*holiday mini kisses treasure cookies*

# macadamia nut white chip pumpkin cookies

**2 cups all-purpose flour**
**2 teaspoons ground cinnamon**
**1 teaspoon ground cloves**
**1 teaspoon baking soda**
**1 cup (2 sticks) butter or margarine, softened**
**½ cup granulated sugar**
**½ cup packed brown sugar**
**1 cup LIBBY'S® 100% Pure Pumpkin**
**1 large egg**
**2 teaspoons vanilla extract**
**2 cups (12-ounce package) NESTLÉ® TOLL HOUSE® Premier White Morsels**
**⅔ cup coarsely chopped macadamia nuts or walnuts, toasted**

**PREHEAT** oven to 350°F.

**COMBINE** flour, cinnamon, cloves and baking soda in small bowl. Beat butter, granulated sugar and brown sugar in large mixer bowl until creamy. Beat in pumpkin, egg and vanilla extract until blended. Gradually beat in flour mixture. Stir in morsels and nuts. Drop by rounded tablespoon onto greased baking sheets; flatten slightly with back of spoon or greased bottom of glass dipped in granulated sugar.

**BAKE** for 11 to 14 minutes or until centers are set. Cool on baking sheets for 2 minutes; remove to wire racks to cool completely.

*Makes about 4 dozen cookies*

# spicy gingerbread cookies

**Cookies**
- ¾ **cup (1½ sticks) butter, softened**
- ⅔ **cup light molasses**
- ½ **cup packed brown sugar**
- 1 **egg**
- 1½ **teaspoons grated lemon peel**
- 2½ **cups all-purpose flour**
- 1¼ **teaspoons ground cinnamon**
- 1 **teaspoon ground allspice**
- 1 **teaspoon vanilla**
- ½ **teaspoon salt**
- ½ **teaspoon baking soda**
- ½ **teaspoon ground ginger**
- ¼ **teaspoon baking powder**

**Frosting**
- 4 **cups powdered sugar**
- ½ **cup (1 stick) butter, softened**
- 4 **tablespoons milk**
- 2 **teaspoons vanilla**
- **Assorted food colorings (optional)**

1. For cookies, combine butter, molasses, brown sugar, egg and lemon peel in large bowl. Beat with electric mixer at medium speed until smooth and creamy. Add all remaining cookie ingredients. Reduce speed to low; beat well. Wrap in plastic wrap; refrigerate at least 2 hours.

2. Preheat oven to 350°F. Roll out dough, one half at a time, on well-floured surface to ¼-inch thickness. (Keep remaining dough refrigerated.) Cut with 3- to 4-inch cookie cutters. Place on greased cookie sheets. Bake 6 to 8 minutes or until firm. Remove immediately to wire racks. Cool completely.

3. For frosting, combine powdered sugar, butter, milk and vanilla in small bowl. Beat with electric mixer at low speed until fluffy. Tint frosting with food colorings, if desired. Decorate cookies with frosting.          *Makes about 4 dozen cookies*

# yule tree namesakes

**Butter Cookie Dough (recipe follows)**
**Cookie Glaze (page 223)**
**Green food coloring**
**1 to 2 tablespoons powdered sugar**
**Assorted candies**
**3 packages (12 ounces each) semisweet chocolate chips, melted**
**1 cup flaked coconut, tinted green***

*To tint coconut, combine small amount of food coloring (paste or liquid) with 1 teaspoon water in large bowl. Add coconut and stir until evenly coated. Add more coloring, if needed.*

1. Preheat oven to 350°F. Prepare Butter Cookie Dough; roll on floured surface to ⅛-inch thickness. Cut out cookies using 3- to 4-inch tree-shaped cookie cutters. Place 2 inches apart on ungreased cookie sheets. Bake 12 to 14 minutes or until edges begin to brown. Remove to wire racks; cool completely.

2. Prepare Cookie Glaze, reserving ⅓ cup; color remaining glaze green with food coloring. Place cookies on wire rack set over waxed paper-lined cookie sheet. Spoon green glaze over cookies.

3. Add powdered sugar to reserved Cookie Glaze until of desired piping consistency. Spoon into pastry bag fitted with small writing tip. Pipe names onto trees as shown in photo. Decorate with candies as desired. Let cookies stand until set.

4. Line 24 mini (1¾-inch) muffin pan cups with foil baking cups. Spoon melted chocolate into prepared muffin cups, filling evenly. Let cups stand until chocolate is very thick and partially set. Place trees upright in chocolate. Sprinkle tinted coconut over chocolate. Let each card stand until set.     *Makes 24 place cards*

# butter cookie dough

**¾ cup (1½ sticks) butter, softened**
**¼ cup *each* granulated sugar and packed light brown sugar**
**1 egg yolk**
**1¾ cups all-purpose flour**
**¾ teaspoon baking powder**
**⅛ teaspoon salt**

1. Combine butter, granulated sugar, brown sugar and egg yolk in medium bowl. Add flour, baking powder and salt; mix well.

2. Cover; refrigerate until firm, about 4 hours or overnight.

*Makes about 2 dozen cookies*

*yule tree namesakes*

# golden kolacky

**½ cup (1 stick) butter, softened**
**4 ounces cream cheese, softened**
**1 cup all-purpose flour**
**Fruit preserves**

1. Combine butter and cream cheese in large bowl; beat until smooth. Gradually add flour to butter mixture, blending until mixture forms soft dough. Divide dough in half; wrap each half in plastic wrap. Refrigerate about 1 hour or until firm.

2. Preheat oven to 375°F. Roll out dough, one half at a time, on floured surface to ⅛-inch thickness. Cut into 2½-inch squares. Spoon 1 teaspoon preserves into center of each square. Bring up two opposite corners to center; pinch together tightly to seal. Fold sealed tip to one side; pinch to seal. Place 1 inch apart on ungreased cookie sheets. Bake 10 to 15 minutes or until lightly browned. Remove to wire racks; cool completely. *Makes about 2½ dozen cookies*

# lemon melts

**½ cup canola oil**
**½ cup (1 stick) butter, melted**
**½ cup packed brown sugar**
**½ cup powdered sugar**
**1 tablespoon lemon juice**
**1 tablespoon vanilla**
**1½ teaspoons almond extract**
**2 cups all-purpose flour**
**½ teaspoon cream of tartar**
**½ teaspoon baking soda**

1. Preheat oven to 350°F. Grease cookie sheets.

2. Beat oil, butter, sugars, lemon juice, vanilla and almond extract in large bowl with electric mixer at medium speed until creamy.

3. Combine flour, cream of tartar and baking soda in separate bowl. Gradually beat into butter mixture until stiff dough forms.

4. Drop dough by rounded tablespoonfuls 2 inches apart onto prepared cookie sheets; flatten gently with fork. Bake 20 minutes or until cookies brown around edges only. Cool cookies on cookie sheets 1 minute. Remove to wire racks; cool completely. *Makes about 40 cookies*

*golden kolacky*

# tea cookies

**3 cups granulated sugar**
**2 cups shortening**
**2 teaspoons vanilla**
**4 eggs**
**5½ cups all-purpose flour**
**4 teaspoons cream of tartar**
**2 teaspoons baking soda**
**½ teaspoon salt**
**1 cup finely chopped almonds, walnuts or pecans**

1. Preheat oven to 375°F.

2. Beat sugar, shortening and vanilla with electric mixer at medium speed until creamy. Add eggs, one at a time, beating well after each addition. Continue beating until mixture is smooth.

3. Sift flour, cream of tartar, baking soda and salt into separate large bowl. Add almonds. Stir into shortening mixture until well blended.

4. Shape dough into walnut-sized balls. Place 2 inches apart on ungreased cookie sheets. Bake 8 to 10 minutes.

5. Cool 2 hours on wire racks.                    *Makes 8 to 9 dozen cookies*

*tea cookies*

# chocolate-frosted lebkuchen

**4 eggs**
**1 cup sugar**
**1½ cups all-purpose flour**
**1 cup (6 ounces) pulverized almonds***
**⅓ cup candied lemon peel, finely chopped**
**⅓ cup candied orange peel, finely chopped**
**1½ teaspoons ground cinnamon**
**1 teaspoon grated lemon peel**
**½ teaspoon ground cardamom**
**½ teaspoon ground nutmeg**
**¼ teaspoon ground cloves**
**Bittersweet Glaze (recipe follows)**

*To pulverize almonds, place in food processor or blender. Process until thoroughly ground with a dry, not pasty, texture.*

1. Beat eggs and sugar in large bowl with electric mixer at high speed 10 minutes. Meanwhile, in separate bowl, combine flour, almonds, candied lemon and orange peels, cinnamon, grated lemon peel, cardamom, nutmeg and cloves. Blend in egg mixture, stirring until evenly mixed. Cover; refrigerate 12 hours or overnight.

2. Preheat oven to 350°F. Grease cookie sheets and dust with flour or line with parchment paper. Drop dough by rounded teaspoonfuls 2 inches apart onto prepared cookie sheets. Bake 8 to 10 minutes or until just barely browned. Do not overbake. Remove to wire racks. Meanwhile, prepare Bittersweet Glaze. Spread over tops of warm cookies using pastry brush. Cool until glaze is set. Store in airtight container. *Makes about 5 dozen cookies*

# bittersweet glaze

**3 squares (1 ounce each) bittersweet or semisweet chocolate, chopped**
**1 tablespoon butter**

Melt chocolate and butter in small bowl over hot water. Stir until smooth.

# chocolate cherry-nut drops

**¾ cup (1½ sticks) butter or margarine, softened**
**1 cup sugar**
**1 egg**
**½ teaspoon vanilla extract**
**¼ teaspoon almond extract**
**1¾ cups all-purpose flour**
**½ cup HERSHEY'S Cocoa**
**½ teaspoon baking soda**
**¼ teaspoon salt**
**⅓ cup water**
**½ cup chopped nuts**
**½ cup finely chopped maraschino cherries, well drained**
**Vanilla Frosting (recipe follows)**
**Candied cherries, quartered or multi-colored sprinkles (optional)**

1. Beat butter and sugar in large bowl until fluffy. Add egg, vanilla and almond extracts; beat until well blended. Stir together flour, cocoa, baking soda and salt; add alternately with water to butter mixture. Stir in nuts and maraschino cherries. Cover; refrigerate dough 2 to 3 hours.

2. Heat oven to 350°F.

3. Lightly grease cookie sheet. Drop dough by slightly heaping teaspoons onto prepared cookie sheet.

4. Bake 9 to 10 minutes or until set. Cool 1 minute; remove from cookie sheet to wire rack. Cool completely. Spread with Vanilla Frosting. Garnish with candied cherries, if desired. *Makes about 3½ dozen cookies*

# vanilla frosting

**2 tablespoons butter or margarine, softened**
**1½ cups powdered sugar**
**1 to 2 tablespoons milk**
**¼ teaspoon vanilla extract**
**⅛ to ¼ teaspoon almond extract**

Beat butter until creamy. Gradually add powdered sugar alternately with milk, beating to spreading consistency. Beat in vanilla and almond extracts.
*Makes about ¾ cup*

# refrigerator cookies

**½ cup sugar**
**¼ cup light corn syrup**
**¼ cup (½ stick) butter, softened**
**¼ cup cholesterol-free egg substitute**
**1 teaspoon vanilla**
**1¾ cups all-purpose flour**
**¼ teaspoon baking soda**
**¼ teaspoon salt**
**Cookie decorations**

1. Beat sugar, corn syrup and butter in large bowl. Add egg substitute and vanilla; mix well. Set aside.

2. Combine flour, baking soda and salt in medium bowl. Add to sugar mixture; mix well. Form dough into 2 (1½-inch-wide) rolls. Wrap in plastic wrap. Freeze 1 hour.

3. Preheat oven to 350°F. Line baking sheets with parchment paper. Cut dough into ¼-inch-thick slices; place 1 inch apart on prepared cookie sheets. Sprinkle with cookie decorations.

4. Bake 8 to 10 minutes or until edges are golden brown. Cool on wire racks.

*Makes about 4 dozen cookies*

**VARIATION:** Add 2 tablespoons unsweetened cocoa powder to dough for chocolate cookies.

*refrigerator cookies*

# holiday triple chocolate yule logs

**1¾ cups all-purpose flour**
**¾ cup powdered sugar**
**¼ cup unsweetened cocoa powder**
**⅛ teaspoon salt**
**1 cup (2 sticks) butter, softened**
**1 teaspoon vanilla**
**1 cup white chocolate chips**
**1 cup chocolate sprinkles or jimmies**

1. Combine flour, sugar, cocoa and salt; set aside.

2. Beat butter and vanilla in large bowl with electric mixer at medium-low speed until fluffy. Gradually beat in flour mixture until well blended. Cover and chill dough at least 30 minutes.

3. Preheat oven to 350°F. Form dough into 1-inch balls. Shape balls into 2-inch logs about ½ inch thick. Place 2 inches apart onto ungreased cookie sheets.

4. Bake 12 minutes or until set. Let stand on cookie sheets 2 minutes; transfer to wire racks; cool completely.

5. Place white chocolate chips in small microwavable bowl. Microwave at HIGH (100%) 45 seconds. Stir chips until completely melted. Place chocolate sprinkles in another small bowl. Dip each end of cooled cookie first into white chocolate and then into chocolate sprinkles. Return to wire racks; let stand until chocolate is set, about 25 minutes.

*Makes about 3 dozen cookies*

*holiday triple chocolate yule logs*

# peanutty cranberry bars

½ cup (1 stick) butter or margarine, softened
½ cup granulated sugar
¼ cup packed light brown sugar
1 cup all-purpose flour
1 cup quick-cooking rolled oats
¼ teaspoon baking soda
¼ teaspoon salt
1 cup REESE'S® Peanut Butter Chips
1½ cups fresh or frozen whole cranberries
⅔ cup light corn syrup
½ cup water
1 teaspoon vanilla extract

1. Heat oven to 350°F. Grease 8-inch square baking pan.

2. Beat butter, granulated sugar and brown sugar in medium bowl until fluffy. Stir together flour, oats, baking soda and salt; gradually add to butter mixture, mixing until mixture is consistency of coarse crumbs. Stir in peanut butter chips.

3. Reserve 1½ cups mixture for crumb topping. Firmly press remaining mixture evenly into prepared pan. Bake 15 minutes or until set. Meanwhile, in medium saucepan, combine cranberries, corn syrup and water. Cook over medium heat, stirring occasionally, until mixture boils. Reduce heat; simmer 15 minutes, stirring occasionally. Remove from heat. Stir in vanilla. Spread evenly over baked layer. Sprinkle reserved 1½ cups crumbs evenly over top.

4. Return to oven. Bake 15 to 20 minutes or until set. Cool completely in pan on wire rack. Cut into bars. *Makes about 16 bars*

# pistachio cookie cups

**½ cup (1 stick) plus 1 tablespoon butter, softened and divided**
**1 package (3 ounces) cream cheese, softened**
**2 tablespoons granulated sugar**
**1 cup all-purpose flour**
**½ teaspoon grated orange peel**
**1 cup powdered sugar**
**½ cup chopped pistachio nuts**
**⅓ cup dried cranberries**
**1 egg**
**½ teaspoon orange extract**
**Additional powdered sugar for garnish**

1. Beat ½ cup butter, cream cheese and granulated sugar with electric mixer at medium speed until light and fluffy. Add flour and orange peel; beat just until blended. Shape into ball; wrap in plastic wrap. Freeze 30 minutes.

2. Combine all remaining ingredients in small bowl; mix well. Set aside.

3. Preheat oven to 350°F. Lightly spray 24 mini muffin cups with nonstick cooking spray.

4. Press 1 tablespoon dough firmly into bottom and up side of each muffin cup. Fill shells ¾ full with pistachio nut mixture.

5. Bake 25 minutes or until filling is set. Remove cookie cups to wire rack; cool completely. Sprinkle with powdered sugar, if desired.     *Makes 2 dozen cookies*

# christmas wreaths

**1 package (18 ounces) refrigerated sugar cookie dough**
**2 tablespoons all-purpose flour**
   **Green food coloring**
   **Green colored sugar or sprinkles**
   **Red decorating icing**

1. Remove dough from wrapper; place in large bowl. Let dough stand at room temperature about 15 minutes.

2. Add flour and green food coloring to dough in bowl; beat with electric mixer at medium speed until dough is well blended and evenly colored. Divide dough in half; wrap both halves in plastic wrap and freeze 20 minutes.

3. Preheat oven to 350°F. Grease cookie sheets. For cookie bottoms, roll 1 dough half on lightly floured surface to ⅜-inch thickness. Cut with 3-inch fluted or round cookie cutter; place 2 inches apart on prepared cookie sheets. Using 1-inch round cookie cutter, cut center circle from each cookie.

4. For cookie tops, roll remaining dough half on lightly floured surface to ⅜-inch thickness. Cut with 3-inch fluted or round cookie cutter; place 2 inches apart on prepared cookie sheets. Using 1-inch round cookie cutter, cut center circle from each cookie. Using miniature cookie cutters or knife, cut tiny circles in cookie tops. Decorate with green sugar or sprinkles as desired.

5. Bake cutouts 10 minutes or until very lightly browned at edges. Cool on cookie sheet 5 minutes; transfer to wire racks to cool completely.

6. To assemble, spread icing onto flat sides of bottom cookies; place top cookies over icing.     *Makes about 1½ dozen sandwich cookies*

*christmas wreaths*

# cozy fireside sips

## viennese coffee

**1 cup heavy cream, divided**
**1 teaspoon powdered sugar**
**1 bar (3 ounces) bittersweet or semisweet chocolate**
**3 cups strong freshly brewed hot coffee**
**¼ cup crème de cacao or Irish cream (optional)**

1. Chill bowl, beaters and cream before whipping. Place ⅔ cup cream and sugar into chilled bowl. Beat with electric mixer at high speed until soft peaks form.

2. Cover and refrigerate up to 8 hours. If mixture has separated slightly after refrigeration, whisk lightly with wire whisk before using.

3. To make chocolate shavings for garnish, place waxed paper under chocolate. Holding chocolate in one hand, make short, quick strokes across chocolate with vegetable peeler; set aside. Break remaining chocolate into pieces.

4. Place remaining ⅓ cup cream in heavy small saucepan. Bring to a simmer over medium-low heat. Add chocolate pieces; cover and remove from heat. Let stand 5 minutes or until chocolate is melted; stir until smooth.

5. Add hot coffee to chocolate mixture. Heat over low heat just until bubbles form around edge of pan and coffee is heated through, stirring frequently. Remove from heat; stir in crème de cacao, if desired.

6. Pour into 4 warmed mugs. Top with whipped cream. Garnish with chocolate shavings. *Makes about 4 (1-cup) servings*

*viennese coffee*

# holiday citrus punch

**Ingredients**
- **1 pint vanilla frozen yogurt, softened**
- **Fresh or frozen raspberries**
- **2 cups cold water**
- **1 can (12 ounces) frozen lemonade concentrate, thawed**
- **1 can (12 ounces) frozen orange-cranberry juice concentrate, thawed**
- **1 can (12 ounces) frozen Ruby Red grapefruit juice concentrate, thawed**
- **¼ cup lime juice**
- **2 bottles (28 ounces each) ginger ale, chilled**

**Supplies**
- **Parchment paper**
- **Assorted cookie cutters in star, snowflake or holiday shapes**

1. Line 9-inch square baking dish with parchment paper. Spread yogurt evenly into prepared dish; freeze until firm. Meanwhile, place baking sheet in freezer to chill.

2. Remove frozen yogurt from baking dish. Using cookie cutters, cut out desired shapes from frozen yogurt. Transfer cutouts to chilled baking sheet. Press raspberry into center of each yogurt cutout; freeze until ready to serve.

3. Combine water, fruit juice concentrates and lime juice in punch bowl. Just before serving, pour in ginger ale. Float yogurt cutouts in punch.

*Makes 24 to 26 servings*

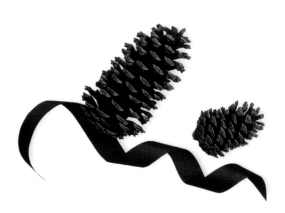

*top to bottom: holiday citrus punch, storefront place cards (page 223)*

# mulled cranberry tea

**2 tea bags**
**1 cup boiling water**
**1 bottle (48 ounces) cranberry juice**
**⅓ cup sugar**
**½ cup dried cranberries (optional)**
**1 large lemon, cut into ¼-inch slices**
**4 cinnamon sticks**
**6 whole cloves**
   **Additional thin lemon slices for garnish**
   **Additional cinnamon sticks for garnish**

## Slow Cooker Directions

1. Place tea bags in slow cooker. Pour boiling water over tea bags; cover and let stand 5 minutes. Remove and discard tea bags. Stir in cranberry juice, sugar, cranberries, if desired, large lemon slices, 4 cinnamon sticks and cloves. Cover; cook on HIGH 1 to 2 hours or on LOW 2 to 3 hours.

2. Remove and discard lemon slices, cinnamon sticks and cloves. Serve in warm mug with additional fresh lemon slice and cinnamon stick. *Makes 8 servings*

**Prep Time:** 10 minutes
**Cook Time:** 2 to 3 hours (LOW) • 1 to 2 hours (HIGH)

*mulled cranberry tea*

# banana nog

**2 cups milk**
**1 large ripe banana, cut into pieces**
**½ cup sugar**
**1 tablespoon cornstarch**
**2 egg yolks***
**⅔ cup light rum**
**¼ cup crème de cacao**
**1 teaspoon vanilla**
**2 cups half-and-half, chilled**
**Whipped cream**
**Unsweetened cocoa powder**
**6 miniature candy canes**

**Supplies**
**Red and/or green ribbon**

1. Process milk and banana in blender or food processor until smooth. Mix sugar and cornstarch in medium saucepan; stir in milk mixture. Heat to simmering over medium heat, stirring occasionally.

2. Lightly beat egg yolks in small bowl; whisk about ½ cup milk mixture into egg yolks. Whisk yolk mixture back into saucepan. Cook over medium heat, stirring constantly, until thick enough to coat back of spoon. *Do not boil.*

3. Remove from heat; stir in rum, crème de cacao and vanilla. Pour into large heatproof pitcher or bowl. Cover; refrigerate until chilled.

4. Just before serving, stir half-and-half into eggnog mixture. Serve in mugs or punch cups; garnish with dollops of whipped cream and sprinkles of cocoa. Tie pieces of ribbon around candy canes; use as stirrers.

*Makes 6 servings (about 6 ounces each)*

# spiced cranberry punch

**2 cups KARO® Light Corn Syrup**
**¼ cup water**
**6 cinnamon sticks**
**2 tablespoons whole cloves**
**½ teaspoon ground allspice**
**2 quarts cranberry juice, chilled**
**1 quart orange juice, chilled**
**1 can (46 ounces) pineapple juice, chilled**
**2 quarts ginger ale, chilled**
**½ cup lemon juice**

1. In medium saucepan combine corn syrup, water, cinnamon sticks, cloves and allspice. Bring to boil over medium-high heat. Reduce heat; simmer 10 minutes.

2. Cover and refrigerate until thoroughly chilled; strain to remove spices.

3. Just before serving, combine spiced syrup, fruit juices, ginger ale and lemon juice.                    *Makes about 36 (6-ounce) servings*

**Prep Time:** 15 minutes, plus chilling

# hot mulled cider

**½ gallon apple cider**
**½ cup packed light brown sugar**
**½ cup applejack or bourbon (optional)**
**1½ teaspoons balsamic or cider vinegar**
**1 teaspoon vanilla**
**1 cinnamon stick**
**6 whole cloves**

**Slow Cooker Directions**

Combine all ingredients in slow cooker. Cover; cook on LOW 5 to 6 hours. Remove and discard cinnamon stick and cloves. Serve hot in mugs.
                    *Makes 16 servings*

# triple delicious hot chocolate

**3 cups milk, divided**
**⅓ cup sugar**
**¼ cup unsweetened cocoa powder**
**¼ teaspoon salt**
**¾ teaspoon vanilla**
**1 cup heavy cream**
**1 square (1 ounce) bittersweet chocolate**
**1 square (1 ounce) white chocolate**
**¾ cup whipped cream**
**6 teaspoons mini chocolate chips or shaved bittersweet chocolate**

**Slow Cooker Directions**

1. Combine ½ cup milk, sugar, cocoa and salt in medium bowl. Beat until smooth. Pour into slow cooker. Add remaining 2½ cups milk and vanilla. Cover; cook on LOW 2 hours.

2. Add cream. Cover and cook on LOW 10 minutes. Stir in bittersweet and white chocolates until melted.

3. Pour hot chocolate into 6 coffee cups. Top each with 2 tablespoons whipped cream and 1 teaspoon chocolate chips. *Makes 6 servings*

# cranberry snow punch

**1 cup apple juice, chilled**
**½ cup superfine sugar**
**1½ cups cranberry juice cocktail, chilled**
**1½ cups bitter lemon or tonic water, chilled**
**1 pint vanilla frozen yogurt**

1. Combine apple juice and sugar in punch bowl; stir until sugar dissolves. Stir in cranberry juice and bitter lemon.

2. Scoop frozen yogurt onto top of punch. Serve immediately.
*Makes 8 servings (about 4 ounces each)*

*triple delicious hot chocolate*

# festive holiday punch

**8 cups MOTT'S® Apple Juice**
**8 cups cranberry juice cocktail**
**2 red apples, sliced**
**2 cups cranberries**
**3 liters lemon-lime soda**
  **Ice cubes, as needed**

Pour apple and cranberry juices into punch bowl. Fifteen minutes before serving, add apple slices, cranberries, soda and ice. Do not stir.          *Makes 24 servings*

# holiday mulled cider

 **6 cups apple cider**
 **3 cups orange juice**
 **2 cups water**
**½ cup freshly squeezed lemon juice**
**¾ cup firmly packed DOMINO® Light Brown Sugar**
 **3 sticks cinnamon**
**12 whole cloves**
**¼ teaspoon ground cardamom**
**¼ teaspoon ground ginger**
**⅛ teaspoon ground nutmeg**
  **Lemon slices**

Combine all ingredients except lemon slices in 4-quart saucepan. Bring to a boil. Reduce heat to low; continue heating for 15 minutes to blend spices. Remove cinnamon sticks and cloves. Serve in mugs garnished with lemon slices.

*Makes 12 servings*

**Preparation Time:** 10 minutes
**Cooking Time:** 15 minutes

*festive holiday punch*

# mocha nog

**1 quart eggnog**
**1 tablespoon instant French vanilla or regular coffee granules**
**¼ cup coffee-flavored liqueur**
 **Whipped cream and chocolate shavings for garnish**

1. Heat eggnog and coffee granules in large saucepan over medium heat until mixture is hot and coffee granules are dissolved. *Do not boil.* Remove from heat; stir in liqueur.

2. Pour eggnog into individual mugs. Garnish with whipped cream and chocolate shavings. *Makes 8 servings*

**Prep and Cook Time:** 10 minutes

# brandied cranapple punch

**1½ quarts (6 cups) cranapple juice cocktail**
**1 small orange, thinly sliced**
**¼ cup firmly packed light brown sugar**
**3 cinnamon sticks**
**12 whole cloves**
**1 cup brandy or cognac**
 **Additional orange slices for garnish (optional)**

Combine all ingredients except brandy and additional orange slices in large saucepan. Bring to simmer over medium heat. Reduce heat to low; add brandy. Ladle into mugs, leaving cinnamon sticks and cloves in saucepan; garnish with sliced oranges, if desired. *Makes 6 to 8 servings*

**Tip:** Punch may be prepared in a crockpot. Combine all ingredients except brandy in a large crockpot; cover and turn heat to high until punch is very hot, about 1 hour. Stir in brandy; turn heat to low. Punch may be kept warm and served from crockpot up to 2 hours.

*mocha nog*

# icy mimosas

**6 cloth napkins (optional)**
**6 wine goblets, preferably chilled**
**3 cups frozen Tropic Ice mix, crushed (recipe follows)**
**3 cups diet ginger ale or champagne**
**6 frozen whole strawberries with stems attached**

Tie napkin around stem of each wine goblet, if desired. Spoon ½ cup crushed Tropic Ice mixture into each goblet. Pour ½ cup diet ginger ale over each serving and add 1 frozen strawberry.                    *Makes 6 servings*

# tropic ice

**4 cups tropical fruit juice, such as pineapple, orange and banana**
**1 (12-ounce) can diet ginger ale**
**¾ cup frozen white grape juice concentrate**
**½ cup dry white wine, such as Chardonnay (see Note)**

1. Place all ingredients in large resealable freezer storage bag. Place in freezer overnight or until frozen.

2. To serve, place bag on counter and, using meat mallet, pound to break up large pieces of frozen mixture or use fork to scrape frozen mixture into slush. Store remaining frozen mixture in freezer until needed. Mixture can be made ahead of time and stored in freezer up to 1 month.                    *Makes about 7 cups*

**NOTE:** The alcohol in the wine keeps the mixture from freezing rock hard. If you choose not to use the wine, the mixture will be harder, but can still be scraped with a fork or broken up with a mallet, after thawing slightly. You can also chop the ice in a food processor to make a slush.

# spiced tea (russian-style)

**1 tub (0.55 ounces) sugar-free lemonade-flavored soft drink mix**
**1 tub (0.55 ounces) sugar-free orange-flavored breakfast**
**beverage crystals**
**1 cup unsweetened iced tea mix**
**1 ½ cups EQUAL® SPOONFUL***
**1 teaspoon ground cinnamon**
**½ teaspoon ground cloves**
**½ teaspoon ground allspice**
**Boiling water**

*\*May substitute 36 packets EQUAL® sweetener.*

● Mix dry ingredients together, stirring well. Measure 2 tablespoons mixture (if prepared with Equal® Spoonful) or 1 tablespoon mixture (if prepared with Equal® packets) into each 8-ounce mug; fill with boiling water and stir to blend.

● Store remaining mixture in covered jar.          *Makes 20 (8-ounce) servings*

# hot buttered cider

**⅓ cup packed brown sugar**
**¼ cup (½ stick) butter, softened**
**¼ cup honey**
**¼ teaspoon ground cinnamon**
**¼ teaspoon ground nutmeg**
**Apple cider or juice**

1. Beat sugar, butter, honey, cinnamon and nutmeg until well blended and fluffy. Place butter mixture in tightly covered container. Refrigerate up to 2 weeks. Bring butter mixture to room temperature before using.

2. To serve, heat apple cider in large saucepan over medium heat until hot. Fill individual mugs with hot apple cider; stir in 1 tablespoon butter mixture per 1 cup apple cider. Garnish as desired.                    *Makes 12 servings*

**Prep and Cook Time:** 15 minutes

# spiced apple tea

**2 cups unsweetened apple juice**
**1 cinnamon stick**
**6 whole cloves**
**3 cups water**
**3 bags cinnamon herbal tea**
**Additional cinnamon sticks (optional)**

1. Combine juice, cinnamon stick and cloves in medium saucepan. Bring to a boil over high heat. Reduce heat to low; simmer 10 minutes. Meanwhile, place water in another medium saucepan. Bring to a boil over high heat. Remove from heat; drop in tea bags and allow to steep 6 minutes. Remove and discard tea bags.

2. Strain juice mixture; discard spices. Stir juice mixture into tea. Serve warm with additional cinnamon sticks, if desired, or refrigerate and serve cold over ice. (Tea may be made ahead and reheated.)                    *Makes 4 servings*

*hot buttered cider*

# hot cranberry-lemon wine punch

    3 cups water
    ¾ to 1 cup sugar
    20 whole cloves
    2 sticks cinnamon
    1 bottle (750 mL) rosé wine
    1 bottle (32 ounces) cranberry juice cocktail
    Juice of 6 SUNKIST® lemons (1 cup)

In saucepot, combine water, sugar and spices. Bring to boil, stirring until sugar dissolves. Reduce heat; simmer 5 minutes. Remove spices. Add remaining ingredients; heat. For garnish, float clove-studded lemon cartwheel slices in punch, if desired.                    *Makes about 11 cups (eighteen 5-ounce servings)*

**COLD CRANBERRY-LEMON WINE PUNCH:** After simmering water, sugar and spices, chill syrup mixture. To serve, in punch bowl combine all ingredients. Add ½ cup brandy, if desired. Add ice or float an ice ring.

# smooth mocha coffee

    ¾ cup hot brewed coffee
    2 tablespoons HERSHEY¦S Syrup
    Whipped cream (optional)
    Ground cinnamon (optional)

Stir together coffee and syrup in mug or cup. Garnish with whipped cream and cinnamon, if desired. Serve immediately.                    *Makes 1 serving*

*hot cranberry-lemon wine punch*

# hot spiced tea

**4 cups freshly brewed tea**
**¼ cup honey**
**4 cinnamon sticks**
**4 whole cloves**
**4 lemon or orange slices (optional)**

Combine tea, honey, cinnamon sticks and cloves in large saucepan; simmer 5 minutes. Serve hot. Garnish with lemon slices, if desired.          *Makes 4 cups*

*Favorite recipe from* **National Honey Board**

# christmas carol punch

**2 medium red apples**
**2 quarts clear apple cider**
**½ cup SUN•MAID® Raisins**
**8 cinnamon sticks**
**2 teaspoons whole cloves**
**¼ cup lemon juice**
   **Lemon slices**
   **Orange slices**

Core apples; slice into ½-inch rings. In Dutch oven, combine cider, apple rings, raisins, cinnamon and cloves. Bring to a boil over high heat; reduce heat to low and simmer 5 to 8 minutes or until apples are just tender. Remove cloves; add lemon juice, lemon slices and orange slices. Pour into punch bowl. Ladle into large mugs, include apple ring, raisins and citrus slices in each serving. Serve with spoons.          *Makes about 8 cups*

# warming winter punch

**1 unpeeled SUNKIST® orange, cut into half-cartwheel slices**
**1 unpeeled SUNKIST® lemon, cut into half-cartwheel slices**
**2 cups water**
**½ cup packed brown sugar**
**4 cinnamon sticks**
**8 whole cloves**
**4 cups freshly squeezed SUNKIST® orange juice**
**2 cups pineapple juice**
**Juice of 2 SUNKIST® lemons**

Place citrus slices in heat-proof bowl or large pitcher. In large saucepan, combine water, sugar, cinnamon and cloves; bring to a boil. Reduce heat and simmer, uncovered, 10 minutes. Add juices and heat. *Do not boil.* Pour over citrus slices; stir well.                                             *Makes about 8 cups*

**NOTE:** Also good chilled and served over ice.

# raspberry wine punch

**1 package (10 ounces) frozen red raspberries in syrup, thawed**
**1 bottle (750 mL) white Zinfandel or blush wine**
**¼ cup raspberry-flavored liqueur**

**For Decorations:**
**Empty half-gallon milk or juice carton**
**3 to 4 cups distilled water, divided**
**Sprigs of pine and tinsel**
**Fresh cranberries**

1. Process raspberries with syrup in food processor or blender until smooth; press through strainer, discarding seeds. Combine wine, raspberry purée and liqueur in pitcher; refrigerate until serving time. Rinse out wine bottle; remove label.

2. Fully open top of carton. Place wine bottle in center of carton. Tape bottle securely to carton so bottle will not move when adding water. Pour 2 cups distilled water into carton. Carefully push pine sprigs, tinsel and cranberries into water between bottle and carton to form decorative design. Add remaining water to almost fill carton. Freeze until firm, 8 hours or overnight.

3. Just before serving, peel carton from ice block. Using funnel, pour punch into wine bottle. Wrap bottom of ice block with white cotton napkin or towel to hold while serving. *Makes 8 servings*

**NOTE:** Punch can also be served in punch bowl if desired.

*raspberry wine punch*

# hot chocolate

**3 ounces semisweet chocolate, finely chopped**
**¼ to ½ cup sugar**
**4 cups milk, divided**
**1 teaspoon vanilla**
**Whipped cream and marshmallows (optional)**

1. Combine chocolate, sugar and ¼ cup milk in medium saucepan over medium-low heat. Cook, stirring constantly, until chocolate melts. Add remaining 3¾ cups milk; heat until hot, stirring occasionally. *Do not boil.* Remove from heat; stir in vanilla.

2. Beat with wire whisk until frothy. Pour into mugs and top with whipped cream and marshmallows, if desired. Serve immediately.     *Makes 4 servings*

**HOT COCOA:** Substitute ¼ cup unsweetened cocoa powder for semisweet chocolate and use ½ cup sugar; heat as directed.

**HOT MOCHA:** Add 4 teaspoons instant coffee to milk mixture; heat as directed.

# chocolate new york egg cream

**1 square (1 ounce) semisweet chocolate (optional)**
**¼ cup chocolate syrup**
**1 cup chilled club soda or carbonated mineral water**
**Ice**

1. Shave chocolate with vegetable peeler, if desired. (Makes about ½ cup.)

2. Pour syrup into 12-ounce glass. Stir in club soda until foamy. Add ice. Garnish with 1 teaspoon chocolate shavings.* Serve immediately.     *Makes 1 serving*

*\*Cover and refrigerate leftover chocolate shavings for another use.*

*left to right: hot chocolate and chocolate new york egg cream*

# dazzling desserts

## easy eggnog pound cake

**1 (18.25-ounce) package yellow cake mix**
**1 (4-serving size) package instant vanilla pudding and pie**
  **filling mix**
**¾ cup BORDEN® EggNog**
**¾ cup vegetable oil**
**4 eggs**
**½ teaspoon ground nutmeg**
  **Powdered sugar (optional)**

1. Preheat oven to 350°F. In large mixing bowl, combine cake mix, pudding mix, Borden® EggNog and oil; beat at low speed of electric mixer until moistened. Add eggs and nutmeg; beat at medium-high speed 4 minutes.

2. Pour into greased and floured 10-inch fluted or tube pan.

3. Bake 40 to 45 minutes or until wooden pick inserted near center comes out clean.

4. Cool 10 minutes; remove from pan. Cool completely. Sprinkle with powdered sugar (optional). *Makes one 10-inch cake*

## apricot cranberry-walnut sugar plums

**½ cup (about 3 ounces) *each* dried apricots and dried cranberries**
**½ cup walnut pieces**
**2 tablespoons plus 2 teaspoons orange liqueur**
**¼ teaspoon ground nutmeg**
**⅔ cup coarse white or colored sugar**

1. Line medium baking dish with waxed paper; set aside.

2. Place apricots, cranberries, walnuts, orange liqueur and nutmeg in food processor; process until mixture is finely chopped and comes together.

3. Place sugar in small bowl. Butter hands lightly. Form fruit mixture into 1-inch balls. Roll in sugar to coat evenly. Place in prepared pan. Let stand 20 to 30 minutes or until firm. Cover tightly and refrigerate up to 3 days. *Makes about 20 balls*

*easy eggnog pound cake*

# holiday pumpkin muffins

**2½ cups all-purpose flour**
**1 cup packed light brown sugar**
**1 tablespoon baking powder**
**1 teaspoon ground cinnamon**
**½ teaspoon ground nutmeg**
**½ teaspoon ground ginger**
**¼ teaspoon salt**
**1 cup solid-pack pumpkin (not pumpkin pie filling)**
**¾ cup milk**
**2 eggs**
**6 tablespoons (¾ stick) butter, melted**
**⅔ cup roasted, salted pepitas (pumpkin seeds), divided**
**½ cup golden raisins**

1. Preheat oven to 400°F. Grease or paper-line 18 (2¾-inch) muffin cups.

2. Combine flour, brown sugar, baking powder, cinnamon, nutmeg, ginger and salt in large bowl. Stir pumpkin, milk, eggs and melted butter in medium bowl until well blended. Stir pumpkin mixture into flour mixture. Mix just until all ingredients are moistened. Stir in ⅓ cup pepitas and raisins. Spoon into prepared muffin cups, filling ⅔ full. Sprinkle remaining pepitas over muffin batter.

3. Bake 15 to 18 minutes or until toothpick inserted into centers comes out clean. Cool in pans 10 minutes. Remove from pans and cool completely on wire racks. Store in airtight container. *Makes 18 muffins*

*holiday pumpkin muffins*

# linzer torte

**½ cup whole almonds, toasted**
**1½ cups all-purpose flour**
**1 teaspoon ground cinnamon**
**¼ teaspoon salt**
**¾ cup granulated sugar**
**½ cup (1 stick) butter, softened**
**½ teaspoon grated lemon peel**
**1 egg**
**¾ cup raspberry or apricot jam**
**Sifted powdered sugar**

1. Process almonds in food processor until ground, but not pasty. Preheat oven to 375°F. Combine flour, almonds, cinnamon and salt in medium bowl; set aside. Beat granulated sugar, butter and lemon peel in large bowl with electric mixer at medium speed about 5 minutes or until light and fluffy, scraping down side of bowl once. Beat in egg until well blended. Beat in flour mixture at low speed until well blended.

2. Spoon ⅔ of dough onto bottom of 10-inch tart pan with removable bottom. Pat dough evenly over bottom and up side of pan. Spread jam over bottom of dough. Roll remaining ⅓ of dough on lightly floured surface into 10×5-inch rectangle. Cut dough into ten ½-inch-wide strips using pizza wheel or sharp knife.

3. Arrange 4 or 5 strips of dough lengthwise across jam. Arrange another 4 or 5 strips of dough crosswise across top. Trim and press ends of dough strips into edge of crust. Bake 25 to 35 minutes or until crust is golden brown. Cool completely in pan on wire rack. Remove torte from pan. Sprinkle with powdered sugar. Cut into wedges. Store, tightly covered, at room temperature 1 to 2 days.

*Makes 12 servings*

*linzer torte*

# fudge meringues

**⅓ cup unsweetened cocoa powder**
**2 tablespoons all-purpose flour**
**1 square (1 ounce) semisweet chocolate, finely chopped**
**3 egg whites**
**¼ teaspoon** *each* **cream of tartar and salt**
**2 cups powdered sugar**

1. Preheat oven to 300°F. Combine cocoa, flour and chocolate in small bowl; set aside. Beat egg whites in medium bowl with electric mixer at high speed until foamy. Add cream of tartar and salt; beat until soft peaks form. Gradually beat in powdered sugar; beat until stiff peaks form. Fold in chocolate mixture.

2. Drop mixture by rounded tablespoonfuls onto cookie sheets lined with parchment paper. Bake 20 minutes or until cookies are crisp when lightly touched with fingertip (cookies will crack). Slide parchment paper onto wire racks; cool completely. Carefully remove cookies from parchment paper. Cookies are best when eaten day they are baked but can be stored in airtight container for up to 2 days. Cookies will become crispier when stored.                *Makes 2 dozen cookies*

# donut spice cakes

**1 package (9 ounces) yellow cake mix**
**½ cup cold water**
**2 eggs**
**½ teaspoon ground cinnamon**
**¼ teaspoon ground nutmeg**
**2 teaspoons powdered sugar**

1. Preheat oven to 350°F. Grease and flour 10 (½-cup) mini Bundt pans.

2. Combine cake mix, water, eggs, cinnamon and nutmeg in medium bowl. Beat with electric mixer at high speed 4 minutes or until well blended.

3. Spoon about ¼ cup batter into each prepared Bundt pan. Bake 13 minutes or until toothpick inserted into centers comes out clean and cakes spring back when touched lightly.

4. Cool in pans on wire racks 5 minutes. Remove cakes from pans. Serve warm or at room temperature. Sprinkle with powdered sugar just before serving.
*Makes 10 servings*

*fudge meringues*

# merry, merry christmas cake

**Cakes & Frostings**
>    **1 recipe Creamy Decorator's Frosting (page 284)**
>    **Green and brown paste food coloring**
>    **1 to 2 tablespoons milk**
>    **2 (8-inch) square cakes**
>    **Fudge Frosting, divided (page 284)**

**Supplies**
>    **1 (19×13-inch) cake board, cut to fit cake if desired, covered**
>    **2 pastry bags with couplers**
>    **Tips: Numbers 3 and 352 or 67**
>    **Tiny bright-colored candies and/or cake decorations**

1. Prepare Creamy Decorator's Frosting; reserve 1¼ cups. Tint ¼ cup frosting bright green and ¼ cup light brown. (To tint frosting, add small amount of desired paste color with toothpick; stir well. Slowly add more color until frosting is desired shade.) Thin remaining Creamy Decorator's Frosting with milk, adding 1 teaspoon at a time, until frosting is thin spreadable consistency.

2. Place one cake layer on prepared board. Prepare Fudge Frosting; spread cake layer with ½ cup frosting; top with second cake layer. Frost entire cake with thinned Creamy Decorator's Frosting to seal in crumbs. Frost again with remaining Fudge Frosting; smooth on top and sides.

3. Use toothpick to outline simple tree shape with trunk in center of cake top. For tree, pipe small leaf with green frosting and number 352 tip, starting at a bottom corner of tree and pointing downward. Pipe another leaf slightly above and overlapping first leaf. Repeat until you have a row of leaves reaching top of tree. Start at other bottom corner; pipe row of leaves on other side. Repeat rows to fill in tree. For tree top, turn cake and pipe 1 leaf, pointing upward. To pipe leaf, hold bag so tip is at 45° angle to the right. Position notch perpendicular to cake. Position opening just above cake and gently squeeze until base of leaf builds up slightly. Continue squeezing while pulling tip out away from base. When leaf is desired length, stop squeezing, then lift tip.

4. For tree trunk, pipe small dots to outline and fill in trunk of tree with light brown frosting and number 3 tip. To pipe dot, hold decorating bag so tip is at 90° angle. Position opening just above cake and gently squeeze. Lift slightly while still squeezing. When dot is desired size, stop squeezing, then lift tip.

5. Decorate tree with candies as desired. For borders, pipe row of leaves around bottom and top with green frosting and number 352 tip.      *Makes 16 servings*

*continued on page 284*

*merry, merry christmas cake*

*merry, merry christmas cake,* continued

## creamy decorator's frosting

**1½ cups shortening**
**1½ teaspoons lemon, coconut, almond or peppermint extract**
**7½ cups sifted powdered sugar**
**⅓ cup milk**

Beat shortening and extract in large bowl with electric mixer at medium speed until fluffy. Slowly add ½ of sugar, ½ cup at a time, beating well after each addition. Beat in milk. Add remaining sugar; beat 1 minute more until smooth and fluffy.* Store in refrigerator. (Frosting may be used for frosting cake and/or piping decorations.)                                                    *Makes about 5 cups*

*\*If frosting seems too soft for piping roses or other detailed flowers or borders, refrigerate for a few hours. Refrigerating frosting usually gives better results, but you may also try stirring in additional sifted sugar, ¼ cup at a time, until desired consistency.*

## fudge frosting

**24 large marshmallows, halved**
**⅔ cup semisweet chocolate chips**
**½ cup shortening**
**½ cup water**
**5 cups sifted powdered sugar**
**3 teaspoons vanilla**

Place marshmallows, chocolate, shortening and water in large saucepan. Cook over low heat until melted and smooth, stirring constantly. Remove from heat; let stand 5 minutes. Gradually beat in sugar and vanilla with electric mixer at medium speed about 6 minutes or until mixture starts to lose gloss. Use frosting immediately.                           *Makes enough to fill and frost 2 (8-inch) square cake layers*

# caribbean christmas ring

**3 tablespoons shortening**
**2½ cups finely chopped California walnuts, divided**
**1 cup all-purpose flour**
**½ cup whole wheat flour**
**1 teaspoon baking powder**
**1 teaspoon baking soda**
**¾ cup (1½ sticks) butter, softened**
**1⅓ cups sugar**
**3 eggs**
**1 cup sour cream or plain nonfat yogurt**
**1 ripe banana, mashed**
**2 tablespoons orange-flavored liqueur**

**ORANGE SUGAR GLAZE**
**1 cup powdered sugar, sifted**
**2 tablespoons orange juice**

**Microwave Directions**

Thoroughly grease 10- to 12-cup microwave-safe Bundt pan with shortening; sprinkle with ½ cup chopped walnuts to coat evenly. Sift flours, baking powder and baking soda into small bowl. In large bowl, beat butter and sugar until fluffy; beat in eggs, one at a time. Stir sour cream or yogurt, banana and liqueur into egg mixture. Fold flour mixture into banana-egg batter; stir in remaining 2 cups walnuts. Spoon into prepared pan and place on top of microwave-safe bowl in microwave, bringing cake up to center of oven. Cook at MEDIUM (50% power) 10 minutes. Continue cooking at HIGH (100% power) 5 to 7 minutes or until cake tests done, turning twice. Let cake stand 15 minutes. Turn out onto serving plate. Let cool.

Mix powdered sugar and orange juice until smooth. Pour glaze evenly over cake and serve. *Makes 20 to 24 servings*

*Favorite recipe from* **Walnut Marketing Board**

# candy cane fudge

**½ cup whipping cream**
**½ cup light corn syrup**
**3 cups semisweet chocolate chips**
**1½ cups powdered sugar, sifted**
**1 cup candy canes, crushed**
**1½ teaspoons vanilla**

1. Line 8-inch baking pan with foil, extending edges over sides of pan.

2. Bring cream and corn syrup to a boil in large saucepan over medium heat. Boil 1 minute. Remove from heat. Stir in chocolate chips; cook until melted, stirring constantly. Stir in powdered sugar, candy canes and vanilla. Pour into prepared pan. Spread mixture into corners. Cover; refrigerate 2 hours or until firm.

3. Lift fudge out of pan using foil; remove foil. Cut into 1-inch squares. Store in airtight container. *Makes about 2 pounds or 64 pieces*

# merri-mint truffles

**1 package (10 ounces) mint chocolate chips**
**⅓ cup whipping cream**
**¼ cup (½ stick) butter**
**1 container (3½ ounces) chocolate sprinkles**

1. Melt chocolate chips with whipping cream and butter in heavy medium saucepan over low heat, stirring occasionally. Pour into pie pan. Refrigerate about 2 hours or until mixture is fudgy, but soft.

2. Shape about 1 tablespoonful of mixture into 1¼-inch ball. Repeat with remaining mixture. Roll balls into uniform round shapes; place on waxed paper.

3. Place sprinkles in shallow bowl. Roll balls in sprinkles; place in miniature paper candy cups. (If coating mixture won't stick because truffle has set, roll between your palms until outside is soft.) Store in airtight container up to 3 days in refrigerator or several weeks in freezer. *Makes about 24 truffles*

*candy cane fudge*

# golden holiday fruitcake

**1½ cups (3 sticks) butter, softened**
**1½ cups sugar**
**6 eggs**
**2 tablespoons fresh lemon juice**
**2 teaspoons grated lemon peel**
**3 cups all-purpose flour**
**2 teaspoons baking powder**
**½ teaspoon baking soda**
**¼ teaspoon salt**
**1½ cups golden raisins**
**1½ cups pecan halves**
**1½ cups red and green candied pineapple chunks**
**1 cup dried apricot halves, cut in half**
**1 cup halved red candied cherries**
**1 cup halved green candied cherries**
**Light corn syrup**
**Candied and dried fruit for garnish**

1. Preheat oven to 325°F. Grease and flour 10-inch round pan. Beat butter in large bowl with electric mixer at medium speed until creamy. Add sugar; beat until light and fluffy. Add eggs, 1 at a time, beating well after each addition. Stir in lemon juice and peel. Combine flour, baking powder, baking soda and salt in large bowl. Reserve ½ cup flour mixture. Gradually blend remaining flour mixture into butter mixture on low speed. Combine raisins, pecans, pineapple, apricots and cherries in large bowl. Toss fruit mixture with reserved ½ cup flour mixture. Stir fruit mixture into butter mixture. Spoon evenly into prepared pan.

2. Bake 1 hour 20 minutes to 1 hour 30 minutes or until toothpick inserted into center comes out clean. Cool in pan 15 minutes. Remove from pan to wire rack; cool completely. Store up to 1 month tightly covered at room temperature. (If desired, cake may be stored wrapped in wine- or brandy-soaked cloth in airtight container. Cake may be frozen up to 2 months.)

3. Before serving, lightly brush surface of cake with corn syrup. Arrange candied and dried fruit decoratively on top. Brush fruit with corn syrup.

*Makes one 10-inch round fruitcake*

*golden holiday fruitcake*

# cherry eggnog quick bread

**2½ cups all-purpose flour**
**¾ cup sugar**
**1 tablespoon baking powder**
**½ teaspoon ground nutmeg**
**1¼ cups prepared dairy eggnog or half-and-half**
**¼ cup (½ stick) plus 2 tablespoons butter, melted and cooled**
**2 eggs, lightly beaten**
**1 teaspoon vanilla**
**½ cup chopped pecans**
**½ cup coarsely chopped candied red cherries**

1. Preheat oven to 350°F. Grease three 5½×3-inch mini-loaf pans.

2. Combine flour, sugar, baking powder and nutmeg in large bowl. Stir eggnog, melted butter, eggs and vanilla in medium bowl until well blended. Add eggnog mixture to flour mixture. Mix just until all ingredients are moistened. Stir in pecans and cherries. Spoon into prepared pans.

3. Bake 35 to 40 minutes or until wooden toothpick inserted into centers comes out clean. Cool in pans 15 minutes. Remove from pans and cool completely on wire rack. Store tightly wrapped in plastic wrap at room temperature.

*Makes 3 mini loaves*

**TIP:** A loaf of homemade bread makes a great gift—especially when it's given in a new loaf pan. Just add a wooden spoon and the recipe, wrap it all up in a festive towel and tie it with ribbon.

*cherry eggnog quick bread*

# country pecan pie

**Pie pastry for single 9-inch pie crust**
**1¼ cups dark corn syrup**
**4 eggs**
**½ cup packed light brown sugar**
**¼ cup (½ stick) butter, melted**
**2 teaspoons all-purpose flour**
**1½ teaspoons vanilla**
**1½ cups pecan halves**

1. Preheat oven to 350°F. Roll pastry on lightly floured surface to form 13-inch circle. Fit into 9-inch pie plate. Trim edges; flute. Set aside.

2. Combine corn syrup, eggs, brown sugar and melted butter in large bowl; beat with electric mixer at medium speed until well blended. Stir in flour and vanilla until blended. Pour into unbaked pie crust. Arrange pecans on top.

3. Bake 40 to 45 minutes or until center of filling is puffed and golden brown. Cool completely on wire rack. Garnish as desired.          *Makes one 9-inch pie*

# white christmas jewel fudge

**3 (6-ounce) packages premium white chocolate chips**
**1 (14-ounce) can EAGLE BRAND® Sweetened Condensed Milk**
**(NOT evaporated milk)**
**1½ teaspoons vanilla extract**
**⅛ teaspoon salt**
**½ cup chopped green candied cherries, if desired**
**½ cup chopped red candied cherries, if desired**

1. In heavy saucepan over low heat, melt chips with EAGLE BRAND®, vanilla and salt. Remove from heat; stir in cherries, if desired. Spread evenly in foil-lined 8- or 9-inch square pan. Chill 2 hours or until firm.

2. Turn fudge onto cutting board; peel off foil and cut into squares. Store covered in refrigerator.          *Makes 2¼ pounds fudge*

**TIP:** Fudge makes a great homemade holiday gift!

*country pecan pie*

# chocolate mint truffles

**1¾ cups (11.5-ounce package) NESTLÉ® TOLL HOUSE® Milk Chocolate Morsels**

**1 cup (6 ounces) NESTLÉ® TOLL HOUSE® Semi-Sweet Chocolate Morsels**

**¾ cup heavy whipping cream**

**1 tablespoon peppermint extract**

**1½ cups finely chopped walnuts, toasted, or NESTLÉ® TOLL HOUSE® Baking Cocoa**

**LINE** baking sheet with wax paper.

**PLACE** milk chocolate and semi-sweet morsels in large mixer bowl. Heat cream to a gentle boil in small saucepan; pour over morsels. Let stand for 1 minute; stir until smooth. Stir in peppermint extract. Cover with plastic wrap; refrigerate for 35 to 45 minutes or until slightly thickened. Stir just until color lightens slightly. (*Do not overmix or truffles will be grainy.*)

**DROP** by rounded teaspoonful onto prepared baking sheet; refrigerate for 10 to 15 minutes. Shape into balls; roll in walnuts or cocoa. Store in airtight container in refrigerator. *Makes about 48 truffles*

**VARIATION:** After rolling chocolate mixture into balls, freeze for 30 to 40 minutes. Microwave 1¾ cups (11.5-ounce package) NESTLÉ® TOLL HOUSE® Milk Chocolate Morsels and 3 tablespoons vegetable shortening in medium, uncovered, microwave-safe bowl on MEDIUM-HIGH (70%) power for 1 minute. STIR. Morsels may retain some of their original shape. If necessary, microwave at additional 10- to 15-second intervals, stirring just until morsels are melted. Dip truffles into chocolate mixture; shake off excess. Place on foil-lined baking sheets. Refrigerate for 15 to 20 minutes or until set. Store in airtight container in refrigerator.

*chocolate mint truffles*

# gingerbread house

**5¼ cups all-purpose flour**
**1 tablespoon ground ginger**
**2 teaspoons baking soda**
**1½ teaspoons allspice**
**1 teaspoon salt**
**2 cups packed dark brown sugar**
**1 cup (2 sticks) plus 2 tablespoons butter, softened and divided**
**¾ cup dark corn syrup**
**2 eggs**
**Meringue Powder Royal Icing (page 298)**
**Assorted gumdrops, hard candies and decors**

### Supplies
**1 (12-inch) square cake board, covered**

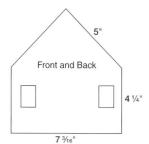

5"

Front and Back

4 ¼"

7 ³⁄₁₆"

**Front:** Cut 1 pattern for front of house. Cut 2 windows.

**Back:** Cut 1 pattern for back of house. Cut 2 windows.

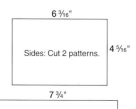

6 ³⁄₁₆"

Sides: Cut 2 patterns.

4 ⁵⁄₁₆"

7 ¾"

Roof: Cut 2 patterns.

6 ¹⁄₁₆"

1. Draw patterns for house on cardboard, using diagrams as guide; cut out.

2. Preheat oven to 375°F. Grease large cookie sheet.

3. Combine flour, ginger, baking soda, allspice and salt in medium bowl.

4. Beat brown sugar and 1 cup butter in large bowl with electric mixer at medium speed until light and fluffy. Beat in corn syrup and eggs. Gradually add flour mixture. Beat at low speed until well blended.

5. Roll about ¼ of dough directly onto prepared cookie sheet to ¼-inch thickness. Lay sheet of waxed paper over dough. Place patterns over waxed paper 2 inches apart. Cut dough around patterns with sharp knife; remove waxed paper. Reserve scraps to reroll with next batch of dough.

6. Bake 15 minutes or until no indentation remains when cookie is touched in center. While cookies are still hot, place cardboard pattern lightly over cookie; trim edges to straighten. Let stand on cookie sheet 5 minutes. Remove cookies to wire racks; cool completely. Repeat with remaining pattern pieces.

7. Prepare Meringue Powder Royal Icing. If desired, some icing may be divided into small bowls and tinted with food coloring to use for decorative piping.

8. Place icing in small resealable plastic freezer bag. Cut off small corner of bag. Pipe icing onto edges of all pieces including bottom; "glue" house together at seams and onto base. Place house on covered cake board.

9. Pipe door, shutters, etc. onto front of house. Decorate as desired with icing and candies. If desired, dust house with sifted powdered sugar to resemble snow.

*Makes 1 gingerbread house*

*continued on page 298*

*gingerbread house*

*gingerbread house,* continued

## meringue powder royal icing

**¼ cup plus 2 tablespoons water**
**¼ cup meringue powder***
**1 box (16 ounces) powdered sugar, sifted**

*Meringue powder is available where cake decorating supplies are sold.*

1. Beat water and meringue powder in medium bowl with electric mixer at low speed until well blended. Beat at high speed until stiff peaks form.

2. Beat in sugar at low speed until well blended. Beat at high speed until icing is very stiff. Cover icing with damp cloth to prevent icing from drying.

**TIP:** This icing is used to glue the house together. It hardens after 5 minutes and completely dries in 20 to 30 minutes.

## mini chocolate cheesecakes

**3 packages (8 ounces each) cream cheese, softened**
**½ cup sugar**
**3 eggs**
**1 teaspoon vanilla**
**8 squares (1 ounce each) semisweet baking chocolate**

1. Preheat oven to 325°F. Lightly grease 12 (2¾-inch) muffin pan cups; set aside.

2. Beat cream cheese and sugar about 2 minutes in large bowl with electric mixer at medium speed until light and fluffy. Add eggs and vanilla; beat about 2 minutes until well blended.

3. Place chocolate in 1-cup microwavable bowl. Microwave at HIGH 1 to 1½ minutes or until chocolate is melted, stirring after 1 minute. Beat melted chocolate into cream cheese mixture until well blended.

4. Divide mixture evenly among prepared muffin cups. Place muffin pan in larger baking pan; place on oven rack. Pour warm water into larger pan to depth of ½ to 1 inch. Bake cheesecakes 30 minutes or until edges are dry and centers are almost set. Remove muffin pan from water. Cool cheesecakes completely in muffin pan on wire rack. *Makes 12 servings*

**MINI SWIRL CHEESECAKES:** Before adding chocolate to batter in mixer bowl, place about 2 heaping tablespoons of batter into each muffin cup. Add chocolate to remaining batter in mixer bowl and beat to combine. Spoon chocolate batter on top of vanilla batter in muffin cups. Swirl with a knife before baking.

# bourbon-laced sweet potato pie

**1 pound (2 medium) sweet potatoes, peeled, cut into 1-inch chunks**
**2 tablespoons butter**
**¾ cup packed brown sugar**
**1 teaspoon cinnamon**
**¼ teaspoon salt**
**2 eggs**
**¾ cup whipping cream**
**¼ cup bourbon or whiskey**
   **Pastry for 9-inch pie (or ½ of 15-ounce package refrigerated
   pastry crusts)**
   **Sweetened whipped cream for serving**

1. Preheat oven to 350°F. Place sweet potatoes in saucepan and cover with water; simmer until very tender, about 20 minutes. Drain well in colander; transfer to large bowl of electric mixer. Add butter; beat at medium speed until potatoes are puréed. Add brown sugar, cinnamon and salt; beat until smooth. Beat in eggs one at a time. Beat in cream and bourbon.

2. Line 9-inch pie plate (not deep-dish) with pastry; flute edges attractively. Pour sweet potato mixture into pie plate. Bake 50 minutes or until knife inserted into center comes out clean. Transfer to wire rack; cool at least 1 hour or more before serving. Serve warm or at room temperature with whipped cream.

*Makes 8 servings*

**TIP:** Pie may be cooled completely, covered and chilled up to 24 hours before serving. Let stand at room temperature at least 30 minutes before serving.

# cranberry cheesecake muffins

**1 package (3 ounces) cream cheese, softened**
**4 tablespoons sugar, divided**
**1 cup reduced-fat (2%) milk**
**⅓ cup vegetable oil**
**1 egg**
**1 package (about 15 ounces) cranberry quick bread mix**

1. Preheat oven to 400°F. Grease 12 muffin pan cups.

2. Beat cream cheese and 2 tablespoons sugar in small bowl until well blended; set aside.

3. Beat milk, oil and egg in large bowl until blended. Stir in quick bread mix just until dry ingredients are moistened.

4. Fill prepared muffin cups ¼ full with batter. Drop 1 teaspoon cream cheese mixture into center of each cup. Spoon remaining batter over cream cheese mixture.

5. Sprinkle batter with remaining 2 tablespoons sugar. Bake 17 to 22 minutes or until golden brown. Cool 5 minutes. Remove from muffin cups to wire rack to cool.

*Makes 12 muffins*

**Prep and Bake Time:** 30 minutes

# special dark® fudge truffles

**2 cups (12-ounce package) HERSHEY'S SPECIAL DARK® Chocolate Chips**
**¾ cup whipping cream**
**Various coatings such as toasted chopped pecans, coconut, powdered sugar, cocoa or small candy pieces**

1. Combine chocolate chips and cream in medium microwave-safe bowl. Microwave at HIGH (100%) 1 minute; stir. If necessary, microwave an additional 15 seconds at a time, stirring after each heating, until chips are melted and mixture is smooth when stirred.

2. Refrigerate 3 hours or until firm. Roll mixture into 1-inch balls. Roll each ball in coating. Cover; store in refrigerator. *Makes about 3 dozen truffles*

*cranberry cheesecake muffins*

# golden leaf pumpkin pie

**1 package (15 ounces) refrigerated pie crust, divided**
**1 can (16 ounces) solid-pack pumpkin**
**1 cup half-and-half**
**3 eggs**
**⅔ cup sugar**
**¼ cup honey**
**2 teaspoons ground cinnamon**
**1 teaspoon ground allspice**
**1 teaspoon ground nutmeg**
**½ teaspoon salt**
**½ teaspoon ground ginger**
**½ teaspoon ground cloves**
**Golden Leaves (recipe follows)**

1. Preheat oven to 425°F.

2. Roll 1 pie crust on floured surface into 10-inch circle; ease into 9-inch pie plate. Trim and flute. Reserve remaining pie crust for Golden Leaves.

3. Combine remaining ingredients except Golden Leaves. Pour into crust.

4. Bake 10 minutes. *Reduce oven temperature to 350°F.* Bake 40 to 45 minutes or until pastry is brown and knife inserted into center comes out clean. Cool. Garnish with Golden Leaves. Refrigerate leftovers.      *Makes 8 to 10 servings*

# golden leaves

**1 refrigerated pie crust, reserved from pie**
**½ cup half-and-half**
**3 tablespoons sugar**

1. Roll pastry on floured surface to ⅛-inch thickness. Cut out leaf shapes. Mark veins in leaves with tip of knife. Roll pastry scraps into rope ¼-inch thick. Cut into 2- to 3-inch pieces and twist to make tendrils.

2. Preheat oven to 400°F. Lay pastry leaves on bottom of inverted flat-bottomed ovenproof bowl so that leaves will have curved shape.* Lay tendrils on ungreased baking sheet. Brush leaves and tendrils with half-and-half; sprinkle with sugar. Bake 10 to 15 minutes or until golden brown. Remove to wire rack; cool completely. Use immediately. Or place leaves in airtight container and place in refrigerator for up to 1 week or freezer for up to 1 month.      *Makes about 12 leaves*

*Leaves may also be baked flat on ungreased baking sheet.*

*golden leaf pumpkin pie*

# banana nut bread

 ½ cup granulated sugar
 2 tablespoons brown sugar
 5 tablespoons margarine
 1⅓ cups mashed ripe bananas (2 medium)
 1 egg
 2 egg whites
 2½ cups all-purpose flour
 1 teaspoon baking soda
 ½ teaspoon salt
 ⅓ cup walnuts

Preheat oven to 375°F. Spray large loaf pan with nonstick cooking spray; set aside.

Beat sugars and margarine in large bowl with electric mixer until light and fluffy. Add bananas, egg and egg whites. Sift together flour, baking soda and salt in medium bowl; add to banana mixture. Stir in walnuts. Pour into prepared loaf pan.

Bake 1 hour or until wooden pick inserted in center comes out clean. Remove from pan. Cool on wire rack 10 minutes. Serve warm or cool completely.

*Makes 1 loaf (16 servings)*

*Favorite recipe from* **The Sugar Association, Inc.**

# ambrosia

 1 can (20 ounces) DOLE® Pineapple Chunks, drained
 1 can (11 or 15 ounces) DOLE® Mandarin Oranges, drained
 1 DOLE® Banana, sliced
 1½ cups seedless grapes
 ½ cup miniature marshmallows
 1 cup vanilla lowfat yogurt
 ¼ cup flaked coconut, toasted

• Combine pineapple chunks, mandarin oranges, banana, grapes and marshmallows in medium bowl.

• Stir yogurt into fruit mixture. Sprinkle with coconut.

*Makes 4 to 6 servings*

**Prep Time:** 15 minutes

*banana nut bread*

# black forest cake

**1 package (2-layer size) chocolate cake mix plus ingredients to prepare mix**
**2 cans (20 ounces each) tart pitted cherries, undrained**
**1 cup granulated sugar**
**¼ cup cornstarch**
**1½ teaspoons vanilla**
**Frosting (recipe follows)**

1. Preheat oven to 350°F. Grease and flour two 9-inch round cake pans; set aside.

2. Prepare cake mix according to package directions. Divide batter between prepared pans. Bake 30 to 35 minutes or until toothpicks inserted into centers come out clean. Cool in pans on wire racks 10 minutes. Remove from pans; cool completely on racks.

3. Meanwhile, drain cherries, reserving ½ cup juice. Combine reserved juice, cherries, sugar and cornstarch in 2-quart saucepan. Cook over low heat until thickened, stirring constantly. Stir in vanilla. Prepare Frosting.

4. Cut each cooled cake layer horizontally in half. Crumble one layer into medium bowl; set aside.

5. Reserve 1½ cups Frosting for decorating cake. Place one cake layer on cake plate. Spread with 1 cup Frosting; top with ¾ cup cherry topping. Top with second cake layer; repeat layers of Frosting and cherry topping. Top with third cake layer. Frost side of cake with remaining Frosting. Pat reserved crumbs onto frosting on side of cake. Spoon reserved frosting into pastry bag fitted with star decorator tip. Pipe around top and bottom edges of cake. Spoon remaining cherry topping onto top of cake. *Makes one 3-layer cake*

**FROSTING:** Combine 3 cups cold whipping cream and ⅓ cup powdered sugar in chilled deep medium bowl. Beat with electric mixer at high speed until stiff peaks form.

# white chocolate cranberry tart

**1 refrigerated pie crust (half of 15-ounce package)**
**1 cup sugar**
**2 eggs**
**¼ cup (½ stick) butter, melted**
**2 teaspoons vanilla**
**½ cup all-purpose flour**
**6 squares (1 ounce each) white chocolate, chopped**
**½ cup chopped macadamia nuts, lightly toasted***
**½ cup dried cranberries, coarsely chopped**

*Toast chopped macadamia nuts in hot skillet over medium heat about 3 minutes or until fragrant.*

1. Preheat oven to 350°F. Place pie crust in 9-inch tart pan with removable bottom or pie pan. (Refrigerate or freeze other crust for another use.)

2. Combine sugar, eggs, butter and vanilla in large bowl; mix well. Stir in flour until well blended. Add white chocolate, nuts and cranberries.

3. Pour filling into unbaked crust. Bake 50 to 55 minutes or until top of tart is crusty and crust is deep golden brown and knife inserted into center comes out clean.

4. Cool completely on wire rack. *Makes 8 servings*

**SERVE IT WITH STYLE!:** Top each serving with a dollop of whipped cream flavored with ground cinnamon, a favorite liqueur and grated orange peel.

**Make-Ahead Time:** up to 2 days before serving

# pretty poinsettia cake

**Cakes & Frostings**
   2 (8-inch) square cakes
      **Creamy Decorator's Frosting (page 284)**
      **Yellow, red and green paste food coloring**
   1 to 2 tablespoons milk
      **Fudge Frosting (page 284)**

**Supplies**
   1 (19×13-inch) cake board, cut to fit cake if desired, covered
   4 pastry bags with couplers
      **Tips: Numbers 3, 13, 32, and 352 or 67**

1. Prepare Creamy Decorator's Frosting; tint ¼ cup pale yellow, ½ cup deep red, ¼ cup green; reserve 2 cups for white frosting. (To tint frosting, add small amount of desired paste color with toothpick; stir well. Slowly add more color until frosting is desired shade.) Thin remaining frosting with milk, adding 1 teaspoon at a time, until frosting is thin consistency.

2. Place one cake on prepared board. Prepare Fudge Frosting; frost top layer of cake with ½ cup frosting. Place second cake on top. Frost top and sides with thinned Creamy Decorator's Frosting to seal in crumbs. Frost again with remaining Fudge Frosting; smooth frosting on top and sides.

3. Mark cake top into 9 squares (about 2½ inches each) with toothpick, using ruler as guide to lightly score edges of each piece.

4. For poinsettia petals, mark center of each square with toothpick, using ruler as guide. Use photo as guide to pipe 8 leaves around each center mark with red frosting and number 352 tip, overlapping base of leaves slightly.

5. For poinsettia centers, pipe 1 dot in center of each poinsettia with yellow frosting and number 3 tip.

6. For poinsettia leaves, pipe 1 leaf on each poinsettia with green frosting and number 352 tip.

7. For border around each square, pipe rows of tiny shells along scored lines in frosting with reserved white frosting and number 13 tip, starting at top and working downward for each line.

8. Pipe bottom and top shell borders with white frosting; switching to number 32 tip.

9. Pipe 1 dot in each corner of bottom border with red frosting; switching to number 3 tip. Pipe leaf on each side of each dot with green frosting and number 352 tip.                                    *Makes 16 servings*

*pretty poinsettia cake*

# METRIC CONVERSION CHART

## VOLUME MEASUREMENTS (dry)

$1/8$ teaspoon = 0.5 mL
$1/4$ teaspoon = 1 mL
$1/2$ teaspoon = 2 mL
$3/4$ teaspoon = 4 mL
1 teaspoon = 5 mL
1 tablespoon = 15 mL
2 tablespoons = 30 mL
$1/4$ cup = 60 mL
$1/3$ cup = 75 mL
$1/2$ cup = 125 mL
$2/3$ cup = 150 mL
$3/4$ cup = 175 mL
1 cup = 250 mL
2 cups = 1 pint = 500 mL
3 cups = 750 mL
4 cups = 1 quart = 1 L

## VOLUME MEASUREMENTS (fluid)

1 fluid ounce (2 tablespoons) = 30 mL
4 fluid ounces ($1/2$ cup) = 125 mL
8 fluid ounces (1 cup) = 250 mL
12 fluid ounces ($1 1/2$ cups) = 375 mL
16 fluid ounces (2 cups) = 500 mL

## WEIGHTS (mass)

$1/2$ ounce = 15 g
1 ounce = 30 g
3 ounces = 90 g
4 ounces = 120 g
8 ounces = 225 g
10 ounces = 285 g
12 ounces = 360 g
16 ounces = 1 pound = 450 g

## DIMENSIONS

$1/16$ inch = 2 mm
$1/8$ inch = 3 mm
$1/4$ inch = 6 mm
$1/2$ inch = 1.5 cm
$3/4$ inch = 2 cm
1 inch = 2.5 cm

## OVEN TEMPERATURES

250°F = 120°C
275°F = 140°C
300°F = 150°C
325°F = 160°C
350°F = 180°C
375°F = 190°C
400°F = 200°C
425°F = 220°C
450°F = 230°C

## BAKING PAN SIZES

| Utensil | Size in Inches/Quarts | Metric Volume | Size in Centimeters |
|---|---|---|---|
| Baking or Cake Pan (square or rectangular) | $8 \times 8 \times 2$ | 2 L | $20 \times 20 \times 5$ |
| | $9 \times 9 \times 2$ | 2.5 L | $23 \times 23 \times 5$ |
| | $12 \times 8 \times 2$ | 3 L | $30 \times 20 \times 5$ |
| | $13 \times 9 \times 2$ | 3.5 L | $33 \times 23 \times 5$ |
| Loaf Pan | $8 \times 4 \times 3$ | 1.5 L | $20 \times 10 \times 7$ |
| | $9 \times 5 \times 3$ | 2 L | $23 \times 13 \times 7$ |
| Round Layer Cake Pan | $8 \times 1 1/2$ | 1.2 L | $20 \times 4$ |
| | $9 \times 1 1/2$ | 1.5 L | $23 \times 4$ |
| Pie Plate | $8 \times 1 1/4$ | 750 mL | $20 \times 3$ |
| | $9 \times 1 1/4$ | 1 L | $23 \times 3$ |
| Baking Dish or Casserole | 1 quart | 1 L | — |
| | $1 1/2$ quart | 1.5 L | — |
| | 2 quart | 2 L | — |

# acknowledgments

**The publisher would like to thank the companies and organizations listed below for the use of their recipes and photographs in this publication.**

ACH FOOD COMPANIES, INC.

American Lamb Council

Dole Food Company, Inc.

Domino® Foods, Inc.

Eagle Brand® Sweetened Condensed Milk

Equal® sweetener

Fleischmann's® Margarines and Spreads

Grandma's® is a registered trademark of Mott's, LLP

Hershey Foods Corporation

The Hidden Valley® Food Products Company

Holland House® is a registered trademark of Mott's, LLP

Lawry's® Foods

© Mars, Incorporated 2005

MASTERFOODS USA

McIlhenny Company (TABASCO® brand Pepper Sauce)

Mott's® is a registered trademark of Mott's, LLP

National Fisheries Institute

National Honey Board

Nestlé USA

Reckitt Benckiser Inc.

The Sugar Association, Inc.

Sun•Maid® Growers of California

Reprinted with permission of Sunkist Growers, Inc.

Unilever Foods North America

Walnut Marketing Board

# recipe index

# general index

**Heidi Tyline King** writes on a variety of decorating and home improvement topics for a number of national magazines. She has also written several books, including *Beautiful Wedding Crafts, All About Paint,* and *Great American Walls and Windows.*

### Craft Designers
Phyllis Dunstan: 16, 26; Walter B. Fedyshyn, AIFD: 81, 89, 94; Bev George: 36; Janelle Hayes: 13, 42; Nancy Wall Hopkins: 24, 34, 44, 49; Allan Howze: 86, 97, 99; Kathy Lamancusa: 91; Lucie Sinkler: 28, 46; Ed Smith, AIFD: Front cover (bottom left), 79, 84; Grace Taormina: 38.

**Hand Models:** Royal Model Management.

**Illustrations:** Denise Hilton Campbell, Connie Formby.

### Photo credits
**Abode UK:** Nina Ewald, 40, 41, 93, 111; Tim Imrie, 8–9, 108; Ian Parry, 98, 103; Trevor Richards, 96 (bottom); **Air and Sky Company:** 18; **Beateworks Inc.:** Tim Street-Porter, 88, 100–101, 124–125; **Brand X Pictures:** Back cover (top),13, 32, 43, 52, 69, 87, 89, 104, 202, 206, 230, 245, 246, 263; **©Corbis:** 47, 81, 116; **Image Club:** 270; **Image Source:** 311; **The Interior Archive:** Fritz von der Schulenburg, 20 (bottom); **©Dennis Krukowski:** 20 (top), 83 (bottom); **Mark Lohman Photography:** 19, 76–77, 78, 83 (top), 96 (top), 104 (bottom), 114, 118, 121; **PhotoDisc:** 106, 107, 136, 172, 223, 269; **Planet Art:** 252.

### Additional Photography
Sacco Productions Limited; Sam Griffith Photography; Silver Lining Digital, Inc.; ©Deborah Van Kirk; Warling Studios: Brian Warling.

All recipes and photographs that contain specific brand names are copyrighted by those companies and/or associations, unless otherwise specified. All recipe photographs *except* that on page 267 copyright © Publications International, Ltd.

DOLE® is a registered trademark of Dole Food Company, Inc.

™/© M&M's, M, and the M&M's Characters are trademarks of Mars, Incorporated.

© Mars, Inc. 2005.

Libby's, Nestlé, and Toll House are registered trademarks of Nestlé.

SUNKIST is a registered trademark of Sunkist Growers, Inc.

Some of the products listed in this publication may be in limited distribution.

**Pictured on the front cover** *(top to bottom):* Apple Stuffed Pork Loin Roast *(page 180)* and Black Forest Cake *(page 306).*

**Pictured on the back cover** *(clockwise from top):* Cherry Eggnog Quick Bread *(page 290),* Mocha Nog *(page 269)* and Holiday Appetizer Puffs *(page 132).*

**Microwave Cooking:** Microwave ovens vary in wattage. Use the cooking times as guidelines, and check for doneness before adding more time.

**Preparation/Cooking Times:** Preparation times are based on the approximate amount of time required to assemble the recipe before cooking, baking, chilling, or serving. These times include preparation steps such as measuring, chopping, and mixing. The fact that some preparations and cooking can be done simultaneously is taken into account. Preparation of optional ingredients and serving suggestions are not included.